CROCHET
THERAPY

This book is dedicated to the memory of the inspiring crocheter Marinke Slump

ABRAMS EDITION
Editor: Cristina Garces
Cover Design: Heesang Lee
Production Manager: Kathleen Gaffney

QUANTUM EDITION
Publisher: Kerry Enzor
Project Editor: Abi Waters
Senior Editor: Philippa Davis
Designer: Blanche Williams of Harper Williams Design
Photographer: Simon Pask
Technical Consultants: Luise Roberts and Claire Crompton
Production Manager: Zarni Win

Library of Congress Control Number: 2015955482

ISBN: 978-1-4197-2111-3

First published in Great Britain by Apple Press in 2016.

Printed and bound in China
10 9 8 7 6 5 4 3 2 1

Abrams products are available at special discounts when purchased in quantity for premiums and promotions as well as fundraising or educational use. Special editions can also be created to specification. For details, contact specialsales@abramsbooks.com or the address below.

ABRAMS
The Art of Books

115 West 18th Street
New York, NY 10011
www.abramsbooks.com

The
Soothing Art *of*
Savoring Each Stitch

CROCHET
THERAPY

———

BETSAN
CORKHILL

Abrams | New York

Contents

ENERGY

Radiating Mandalas   36   Sun Salutation Yoga Mat Bag 40

RELAX

Wave Wrap   50   Meditation Seat Pillow   53

Project selector

CALM

Calming Mandalas   28   Comforting Pillow   31

EXPLORE

Sleep Tight Eye Mask Set 58   Safe Document Wallet   61

Introduction

In this busy world, we often struggle to find moments of calm where we can focus solely on our own well-being. Stress, anger, anxiety, and lack of confidence are all hallmarks of the hectic lives we often lead. It has been proven again and again that carving out still moments of mindful reflection is essential to keeping us healthy both physically and emotionally, and to improve our productivity and mental agility.

This book aims to show you how simple it is to set aside that precious "you" time: All you need is a hook and some yarn. With simple step-by-step wellness exercises and beautifully inspiring crochet patterns, you will be tapping into your creative nature in no time, all while discovering how to use the calming rhythmic practice of crochet to inspire a more mindful way of life.

As a crocheter, you already know that it makes you feel good. You can, however, learn to enhance those benefits and use crochet to deliberately improve your well-being. Having this knowledge will help you to ride life's inevitable storms and to live well despite them.

I have to confess, I don't crochet that well! The good news is that you don't need to be an expert to reap its benefits; so whether you are a beginner or an expert, a bit of crochet therapy can work wonders.

Enjoy a visualization exercise that takes you on a seashore stroll, some mindful moments to reflect on, relaxation, motivation, and even a bit of daydreaming.

The exercises in this book will give you the tools to manage a range of issues. Different challenges require different life skills, so I have designed a variety of exercises from which you can pick and choose what is most useful to you— enjoy a visualization exercise that takes you on a seashore stroll, some mindful moments to reflect on, relaxation, motivation, and even a bit of daydreaming. (Yes, you have permission to stop, sit down, crochet, and daydream.) Sounds like a good combination to me.

Learning to crochet and knit was a transformative experience for me. The exercises in this book are based on the knowledge I have accumulated over the years as a clinician, well-being coach, and researcher, but also over my years as a maker.

When I was younger I lived life without thinking much about actively taking responsibility for my own well-being or health. Now, I know this is essential if I want to stay well into older age. It took my mother's death for me to realize my own mortality, and after she passed away, I vowed that I would learn to enjoy each moment. That decision led me to investigate mindfulness and its potential benefits.

Mindfulness has enjoyed a surge in popularity following research into its benefits for a range of medical conditions. At its core is the practice of simply being in the moment: practicing non-judgmental awareness of the present moment. Linking mindfulness practice to an activity is a good way to start training a keen mind. Being fully aware of the process of crochet can be a metaphor for fully enjoying the journey of life. Experiencing the moment means you are fully appreciating each activity. (More about mindfulness on page 17.)

My research into the benefits of knitting and crochet suggests that its two-handed, cross body nature is important. Such complex patterns of movement take up a lot of brain capacity so you have less available for mulling over problems or other issues detrimental to well-being. You can enhance crochet's benefits by ensuring you involve the non-hook holding hand more. It's also good to take regular breaks, every 30 minutes or so, to stretch your hands. You will find more on this subject on pages 22–23.

Once you are ready, choose an exercise that speaks to you and prepare to reap the rewards of creative therapy. The exercises begin with therapeutic techniques to be practiced separately from crocheting, with accompanying projects that help reinforce the wellness lesson, and then progress to exercises that have been designed to be practiced while crocheting—but you can jump in wherever. Take your time to reflect on each exercise as you create your projects and enjoy the process of crafting something both beautiful and inspirational.

I promise that you will be hooked in no time.

> Choose an exercise that speaks to you and prepare to reap the rewards of creative therapy.

How to Use This Book

This book is a unique collection of 10 feel-good exercises, each accompanied by two crochet projects that further enhance the craft's benefits to your well-being. They will help you discover how to use crochet as a tool to transform your emotional state and bring moments of calm to your everyday life.

Before you begin each exercise, take time to read through it and the accompanying pattern entirely. Some projects suggest you use the exercise **before** you begin to crochet, while in others you perform the exercise **as** you crochet. In these cases, you may find it helpful to record the words onto your phone, or a recording device, to play back as you work on your related project.

THE EXERCISES

Each of the exercises in this book focuses on a particular aspect of well-being and draws on a range of therapeutic techniques including mindfulness, visualization, relaxation, daydreaming, and motivation (see pages 17–19). To help guide you, each exercise is labeled according to the therapeutic technique it draws on. You can work through the exercises in order, or choose one that deals with an issue you particularly want to address, such as tackling stress at work or building confidence.

A bonus of these exercises is they can be used over and over again—much like the beautiful creations that accompany them. Together with your crocheted projects, they provide you with tools for living your fullest life.

THE PROJECTS

There are 20 beautiful projects in this book, each one designed to further enhance the therapeutic exercise it follows. They also serve a purpose to remind you of how you felt during the exercise and this, in turn, will help you to recall the process. Check out the Feel-good Tips at the end of each project to see how the project can help support the exercise you have just done (see an example opposite).

HOW TO CROCHET

On pages 114–130, you will find a guide to all the stitches used in the book, as well as tips on reading the patterns and getting started. Whether you are new to crochet or have been hooked for years, it is useful to have a read through this chapter before your start your project to familiarize yourself with the stitches and techniques you will be using.

NOTES ON THE PROJECTS

Gauge: For many of these projects, the gauge doesn't matter. Some projects, however, will need to be made with a tight tension. For these projects it is useful to check your gauge before beginning, to ensure perfect results.

Other Materials: Any other materials required for the project, including sewing equipment and backing fabrics, are listed in the You Will Need panel at the beginning of the project.

Yarn: The type of yarn is specified for each project along with the suggested colors. See pages 140–141 for a comprehensive list of yarns used in the book.

Friendship Quilt

Ask each friend to create one large flower in their favorite colors. Work together to make lots of small flowers to link your individual creative selves in a timeless quilt that can be added to at any time.

YOU WILL NEED
● Worsted-weight wool blend yarn, (approx. 1¾ oz/50 g; 98 yds/90 m), 2 balls each in
MC yellow
CCa pink
CCb light pink
CCc blue
CCd green
CCe maroon
● Size H-8 (5 mm) hook
● Yarn needle

GAUGE
Gauge is not important in this project.

DIMENSIONS
Approximately 20" (51 cm) square.
The quilt can be added to at any time, and can be made to any desired size.

TO MAKE A LARGE FLOWER
Using MC, ch4, sl st into first ch to form a ring.
Round 1: ch1, 12sc into ring, sl st into first sc to join. (12 sts)
Round 2: ch3 (counts as first dc), 1dc into base of beg ch-3, 2dc into each st to end of round, sl st into top of beg ch-3 to join. (24 sts)
Fasten off MC. Join in CC of choice.
Round 3: *ch3, [yrh, insert hook into same st, yrh, pull up a loop as tall as the ch-3] 3 times, into next st [yrh, insert hook, yrh, pull up a loop as tall as the ch-3] 3 times, yrh and draw through all 13 loops on hook, ch2, sl st into next st; rep from * 11 times more. (12 puff-petals)
Fasten off and weave in loose ends.

TO MAKE A SMALL FLOWER
Using MC, ch4, sl st into first ch to form a ring.
Round 1: ch1, 12sc into ring, sl st into first sc to join. (12 sts)
Fasten off MC. Join in CC of choice.
Round 2: *ch3, [yrh, insert hook into same st, yrh, pull up a loop as tall as the ch-3] 3 times, into next st [yrh, insert hook, yrh, pull up a loop as tall as the ch-3] 3 times, yrh and draw through all 13 loops on hook, ch2, sl st into next st; rep from * 5 times more. (6 puff-petals)
Fasten off and weave in loose ends.

FINISHING
To assemble the quilt
Lay flowers face down and position them so that they fit together nicely. Using one of the CC colors from the flowers you are joining, loop a short length of yarn around the ch-2 or ch-3 of each adjacent petal and tie them together with a knot. Trim the ends to approximately ½" (12 mm). Repeat this around every petal.

Feel-good tip

Why not create this with your crochet friends? Get together to make the individual flowers then knot them together as a symbol of your friendship.

FRIENDSHIP QUILT **105**

Special Stitches: Advanced or unique crochet stitches are explained at the beginning of each project.

Tips and Notes: Be sure to read any tips or notes before your start your project.

Feel-good Tip: At the end of each project is a suggestion for ways in which you can use your project to develop the exercise further.

Chapter 1
Crochet as Therapy

Nurture Your Creative Mind

This chapter explores how craft can be used as a tool to develop a healthier, calmer, more creative brain, and enhance overall well-being by promoting positive lifestyle changes. By simply picking up your crochet hook, you can be one step closer to achieving a more balanced, mindful life.

My research into the meditative, creative, and social benefits of knitting and crafts has led me down several interesting paths. I've explored the world of neuroscience, well-being, meditation, psychology, and the importance of supportive social engagement and community, to name but a few.

The most life-changing discovery I've made along the way is that each of us has the power to change our body's chemistry, even the wiring of our brain. I think that's a pretty mind-blowing fact—one that has changed my life for the better and it can change yours, too.

Crochet therapy is about enhancing the benefits of your craft and learning to use crochet as a tool to nurture a healthier, curious, and more creative brain.

Your nervous system (including your brain) changes with every experience you remember. It's called neuroplasticity. Gone are the days when it was believed that the brain had a fixed number of cells, reached a peak in your mid-twenties, and declined from there. We now know that new brain cells can be born and new neural pathways opened and strengthened even in old age. That's pretty exciting. However, it's up to you to make this happen. What is certain is that if you sit doing nothing, the brain declines. It's the classic "use it or lose it" scenario.

Even more exciting is the discovery that all our body systems are closely entwined—a change in one will trigger a change in another. For example, your stress system is closely tied into pain and your immune system. This explains why you can seem to catch every bug around when you're highly stressed. By managing stress you can affect positive change throughout your body. Crochet provides you with an ideal tool for doing this and its portability means you can use it whenever and wherever you need to.

OUR CHANGING BODY

"Bioplasticity" describes your body's ability to change. We are all changing all of the time as a result of the experiences we have. You have the power to influence these changes positively by learning new skills, seeking variety, practicing cardiovascular exercise, maintaining a good diet, engaging in activities you enjoy, sustaining supportive social contact, and cultivating community. Crochet can be a valuable tool to facilitate this positive change. It provides a large source of new techniques to explore, enjoyment in the process, and can give you an ongoing means of meeting new people from a wide range of different backgrounds and cultures. Crochet opens up the world and its many opportunities.

WHOLE-PERSON HEALTH

I have been a passionate advocate of whole-person health and well-being since the 1970s and have incorporated this knowledge and outlook into my clinical practice for years.

Well-being is multi-faceted. It is affected by everything you do in life, the people around you, your environment, and everything that happens to you. Life events can and will change you on both a mental and physical level. Because of that, any attempt to improve well-being needs to take into account both physical and mental health. This "whole life" approach in turn gives us many ways of improving well-being, of positively affecting our minds and bodies, and for building reserves and resilience along the way. Life's challenges will affect us all and although you have no control over what life throws at you, you can control your response.

Crochet can be an effective tool to help you on the way to whole-person health. It can teach you valuable life skills such as patience, perseverance, and planning. It gives you a tool to manage your emotions when times get rough. It can lift your mood when you feel down, make you smile when you feel sad, and be your friend when you feel lonely. Use your craft to keep stress levels low or to conquer addictive habits such as smoking or snacking.

The sense of belonging somewhere is important to well-being. Crocheting with others will help you build a supportive network of friends—your community. As a crocheter, you will always belong to the wider crochet community. Even better, groups local to you will provide you with a safe environment to meet new friends from a wide range of backgrounds. Research has shown that supportive friends help us to feel happier and even live longer. Friends support each other through life's ups and downs.

On the flip side, feelings of loneliness are detrimental to health and well-being. Becoming engrossed in an absorbing crochet project can help you enjoy and find peace in moments of solitude rather than allowing them to have a negative effect, so alongside helping you to build your supportive community, crochet will provide you with a means of transforming those times when you feel alone into a positive experience: some "me" time! All of these things will make you stronger and more able to deal with life's challenges.

How the Exercises Work

Based on my years of clinical experience and research into how each of us can influence our health and well-being, I have designed a variety of exercises that incorporate mindfulness, visualization, relaxation, daydreaming, and motivation. Each can play a part in improving your well-being.

WHAT IS MINDFULNESS?

Mindfulness is a type of meditative practice that has been widely publicized for its health benefits. There are thousands of different meditative practices that include those of focused attention, open monitoring, and effortless presence. Each can be beneficial to well-being. However, they do require a period of sustained learning, understanding, and commitment. Crocheters appear to enter a meditative-like state as a side effect of their craft, making the benefits easier to access.

It is possible to enter different mind states depending on the type of pattern you choose. The exercises and projects in this book have been designed to reflect this. For example, a complicated pattern will focus your attention onto each stitch, while during an easy repetitive one you will be "effortlessly present."

Mindfulness is in the open monitoring group of meditations and has a widely researched evidence base for improving well-being. Its practice has been part of a number of religions for thousands of years and it is an essential element of Buddhism. However, you don't have to be religious to use it or to benefit from it. Clinician and researcher Jon Kabat-Zinn introduced mindfulness into Western clinical practice in 1979 when he founded the Mindfulness-Based Stress Reduction program (MBSR).

Mindfulness involves centering your awareness on the present moment in an intentional, non-judgmental way—noticing and observing your thoughts, emotions, and physical sensations. You use the rhythm of your breathing to anchor you in the here and now. If thoughts of the past or future arise, your focus is intentionally brought back to the gentle in/out of breath occurring in the present moment. This process enables you to be fully aware of each moment, and of life as a collection of moments—it makes living a richer experience. Some liken it to waking up to life or seeing the moment with beginner's eyes.

Myths About Mindfulness

One of the most widespread myths about mindfulness is that it always promotes relaxation. Unfortunately it isn't always the case, especially in the short term. The practice centers on the acceptance of your thoughts, emotions, and sensations and learning to let them go. This can include thoughts, emotions, or sensations that may be unpleasant. There has to be a willingness to notice the unpleasant or difficult and to be open to whatever arises.

With practice you can switch off the stress response to problems that arise to enable your body's natural healing system to kick in faster and a feeling of calm to develop in place of a tense, stressed-out one. Learning to accept adverse experiences helps you to respond in a measured way rather than reacting uncontrollably.

Mindfulness isn't a process of emptying your mind, either. On the contrary, it's one of being aware of everything going on in your mind, body, and the space around you. Neither is it about positive thinking or having a particular religious belief. You can learn to live mindfully whatever your background and culture.

WHY MINDFULNESS IS A BENEFIT

Mindfulness is a great antidote to our fast-paced, technology-based lives. These days it can be so easy to live in a blur of activity that it can often mean you miss out on life itself—the here and now. Anxious thoughts usually focus on past events or what the future has in store. In the here and now, neither the past nor future exist. Focusing on the present moment can therefore reduce anxiety.

Research has shown that the regular practice of mindfulness is beneficial to health and well-being in many ways—to reduce stress, manage life's challenges, nurture kindness toward oneself and others, and promote a longer, more enjoyable life. Mindfulness-based practices have been adopted by the medical world to treat conditions such as stress, anxiety, depression, and pain management. For example, while those who practice mindfulness still experience stress, they are less likely to react or be overcome by it. Practiced regularly, mindfulness can actually change your brain on a physical level and benefit you in powerfully positive ways.

INTRODUCING VISUALIZATION

Pain specialists use visualization of movement as a way of sharpening movement maps in the brain. Athletes use it to improve their performance—injured golfers, for example, use it to perfect their swing without moving a muscle. You can use it to improve your well-being too. Practice visualizing the process of crocheting when you want to achieve a calm frame of mind. Even if you don't have your crochet available—before interviews or exams, for example—this process can help you to achieve calm, steady thoughts.

USING RELAXATION

Regular relaxation is good for your mental and physical well-being. The accumulation of stress chemicals has a habit of creeping up on you without you noticing. It can also be easy to forget what it feels like to be truly relaxed—the feeling of stress can quickly become a "normal" state of mind. Your body's natural healing system is powerful but it's considerably dampened, even put on hold, when your stress levels are high. Keeping your stress levels down with a dose of daily crochet will enable your healing system to do its job.

THE POWER OF DAYDREAMING

A bit of daydreaming can be beneficial, too. It gives your mind a mini break from the stresses and strains of life, enabling you to feel refreshed. In eliminating the restrictions and demands of daily life, daydreaming enables your ideas to grow and develop, stimulating creative thought, problem solving, and valuable self-discovery. It's good to give yourself permission to daydream!

SAY YES TO MOTIVATION

We all have days when we can't muster the motivation to do much at all. I've included an energizing exercise to motivate you in these moments (see page 35). Use the exercise whenever you need a bit of "oomph" or confidence to face the world with a smile.

The physical act of smiling is good for you even if you don't feel like it. Lifting the corners of your mouth lifts your mood too. Think of your Wake Up Happy Washcloths and smile as you do so (see page 95). It's incredible what an effect such a simple thing can have.

Crochet Therapy
Crocheting in a mindful way is a good way to introduce the practice into your life. Try seeing your crochet with beginner's eyes. Use all of your sensations to enhance the experience. Marvel at the yarn colors and textures and the means by which a beautiful fabric can be created with a simple hook and string.

Adapting Your Crochet Technique

You can further enhance crochet's benefits by changing the way you crochet a little.

It's known that two-handed, coordinated patterns of movement that cross the midline of the body take up a lot of brain capacity. The brain can't fully focus on two things at a time, so the more absorbing the task, the less capacity it has to pay attention to issues that are detrimental to your well-being.

We all have slightly different ways of crocheting, whether it's the way we hold the hook or the balance between the hand movements. You may already be using both hands equally in your technique, but if not, try feeding the yarn more actively so that both hands are moving well in a coordinated pattern of rhythmic movement. (You can find an overview of basic techniques on pages 110–137.)

Your choice of yarn color and texture can affect your mood, too. My research found that texture is twice as significant as color for affecting mood, so choose a yarn that feels good to touch because it will make you feel good. Even better, combine it with one of your favorite colors to maximize the benefits. The colors you choose will not only affect your mood but also be affected by your mood. In the Everlasting Afghan (see page 80), I've suggested you change the color and texture of your yarn to match your mood of the moment—use it as a way of telling your story.

The 3D movement patterns combined with the tactile nature of your craft are an important contrast to any 2D, screen-based work. If your day is spent in front of a screen, crochet will give you an important means of finding balance.

You can also use the exercises in this book independently of your craft, so please make full use of them in your day-to-day life. I love the way the projects link to the exercises and how the completed items can be used to help you to recall the exercises. The sight of your finished projects can remind you to pick up your crochet or your happy crochet thoughts to manage the here and now whenever you need to.

THE BENEFITS OF STRETCHING

Crochet therapy isn't about getting you to sit down all day crocheting. It's about taking responsibility for your own health and well-being and using crochet as a convenient, effective tool as part of your well-being toolbox. It's about helping you to realize that your well-being is affected by everything you do and that you have the power to improve it.

Sitting for long periods is detrimental to your health regardless of how much exercise you do. It affects your circulation, oxygen input, posture, digestion, joints, and muscles to name but a few. For this reason, an important element of crochet therapy includes regular stretching and moving whenever you can. Movement is essential to keeping well.

It's a good idea to get up to move around for a few minutes every 30 minutes. Take the opportunity to focus your eyes on a distant object to prevent eyestrain. If you spend much of your day sitting because of your work or a disability, talk to a physiotherapist about specific stretching exercises to incorporate into your day.

Crochet involves holding the hook with a pincer grip along with repetitive turning of the hook-holding hand. This combination can mean some people need to pace their activity to avoid hand pain. It's highly advisable that when you take your 30-minute break, you use that time to stretch your fingers and hands, too.

Choose two or three movements from each of the two groups of exercises on the following page. Alternate between them whenever you take a break. Repeat each exercise slowly, five times. Don't force the movements and talk to your health care advisor if you have mobility problems or pain. This will ensure you can continue to enjoy and benefit from your crochet into the future.

Basic Exercises

UPPER LIMB AND HAND EXERCISES

1. Intertwine the fingers of both hands and stretch your arms out in front of you. Lift your arms and stretch upward. Hold for a moment then lower your arms. Follow these movements with your eyes and head.

2. Place your hands together as if in prayer, with your elbows out to the sides. Gently push the heels of your hands together to stretch your wrists.

3. Circle your hands from your wrists, clockwise, then counter-clockwise.

4. Make two fists then stretch out your hands smoothly and fully.

5. Place your hands on your lap, stretch your fingers apart as wide as they will go, then bring them together.

6. Lay your hands on your lap and wiggle your fingers as if you are playing the piano.

HEAD AND NECK EXERCISES

1. Gently roll your shoulders and ease your shoulder blades back. Keeping your head straight, gently tuck your chin in.

2. Imagine there is a thin string coming out of the top of your head. Feel it pulling gently upward, easing and elongating your neck and spine. Relax your mouth and jaw.

3. With your eyes and ears facing forward, take your left ear to your left shoulder in a side bend. Repeat on the right.

4. With your eyes and ears level and facing forward, slowly turn your head from side to side.

5. Tilting your head upward, lift your eyes to the sky, then lower your eyes to the floor, tilting your head downward.

As a crocheter you have the perfect tool to improve your well-being. Crochet therapy can enhance the benefits of living in the moment and your journey through life. Enjoy your crocheting!

Chapter 2
The Projects

Calm

Find a comfortable, calm place to sit or lie. Begin with five minutes for this exercise, gradually building up to 20 minutes. Set a timer with a gentle reminder for when this time is up.

1 Close your eyes and focus on your thoughts.

2 Visualize throwing a smooth, round pebble into a calm pond and observe the circular ripples it creates as they gently undulate outward. Imagine yourself at the center of such calm.

3 Be mindful of your thoughts. Pay attention to them but don't pass judgement—they are simply floating through your mind, much like the ripples on that pond. Observe them entering your mind, then gently floating through and out.

4 If you find yourself passing judgement, gently bring your thoughts back to the ripples on the pond. Let those thoughts quietly float away.

5 Be conscious of the space you occupy and observe those ripples of calm flowing out to fill the space around you. They quietly lap at the edge of objects in their path and gently ripple into infinity. Simply notice this and "just be" with this awareness.

6 You are the center of calm. Be fully aware of this comforting realization. Stay with this sensation until your gentle reminder sounds.

7 Open your eyes and spend a moment recalling the sense of deep tranquillity—simply feeling that center of calm.

8 When you have done this enough times, you will be able to take a few minutes out of your busy life whenever and wherever you feel in need of a sanctuary to calm your mind—even in a busy office.

9 Enjoy being in calm control.

Calming Mandalas

Use this simple pattern to create a series of mandalas to remind you to stay calm.
As well as making beautiful decorations for the home, these pieces can be carried
with you as gentle reminders to take a break.

YOU WILL NEED

* Scraps of DK-weight, wool blend yarns in light blue, mid-blue, and dark blue
* Size D-3 (3.25 mm) hook
* Size E-4 (3.5 mm) hook
* Yarn needle

GAUGE

* Solid mandala: Rounds 1–4 measure 1½" (3.5 cm) in diameter, using a size D-3 (3.25 mm) hook.
* Duo-tone mandala: Rounds 1–4 measure 1¾" (4.5 cm) in diameter, using a size E-4 (3.5 mm) hook.

DIMENSIONS

* Solid mandala: 4½" (11.5 cm) diameter, from point-to-point.
* Duo-tone mandala: 5½" (14 cm) diameter, from point-to-point.

NOTE

Gauge is not important in this project. Using a larger hook makes larger, slightly more relaxed mandalas. Using a smaller hook makes firmer mandalas, ideal for hanging without wall support.

TO MAKE A DUO-TONE MANDALA

Using size E-4 (3.5 mm) hook and first color of yarn, ch4, sl st into fourth ch from hook to form a ring.

Round 1: ch1, 6sc into ring, sl st into first st to join. (6 sts)

Round 2: ch1, 1sc into base of beg ch-1, [ch3, 1sc into next st] 5 times, ch1, 1dc (counts as ch-3 sp) into first st at beg of round to join. (6 sts, 6 ch-3 sp).

Round 3: [ch4, 1sc into next ch-3 sp] 5 times, ch2, 1dc (counts as ch-4 sp) into first st at beg of round to join. (6 sts, 6 ch-4 sp)

Round 4: [ch5, 1sc into next ch-4 sp] 5 times, ch5, sl st into dc st of previous round to join. (6 sts, 6 ch-5 sp)

Fasten off yarn. Join in second color of choice into any ch-5 sp.

Round 5: ch3 (counts as first dc), 5dc into ch-5 sp at base of beg ch-3, [6dc into each ch-5 sp] 5 times, sl st into top of beg ch-3 to join. (36 sts)

Round 6: ch3 (counts as first dc), 1dc into next st, 2dc into next st, [1dc into each of the next 2 sts, 2dc into next st] 11 times, sl st into top of beg ch-3 to join. (48 sts)

Fasten off yarn. Join in first color choice into any dc st.

Round 7: ch1, 1sc into base of beg ch-1, [ch3, skip 1 st, 1sc into next st] to last st, ch1, 1dc (counts as ch-3 sp) into first st at beg of round to join. (24 sts, 24 ch-3 sp)

Round 8: repeat Round 3, working pattern rep 23 times. (24 sts, 24 ch-4 sp)

Round 9: repeat Round 4, working pattern rep 23 times. (24 sts, 24 ch-5 sp)

Fasten off yarn. Join in second color choice into any ch-5 sp.

OPPOSITE Clockwise from top: solid mandalas in light blue, mid-blue, and dark blue; duo-tone mandalas in a combination of light blue, mid-blue, and dark blue.

Round 10: ch1, [2sc, ch3, 2sc] into each ch-5 sp to end of round, sl st into first st at beg of round to join.

Fasten off. Weave in loose ends.

To make a hanging loop

Attach the yarn of choice through the back of a single crochet stitch on the penultimate round. Chain 12, or work a chain of the desired loop length, slip stitch into the back of the same single crochet stitch. Weave in ends. Alternately, you can hang your mandala using the loops created by the last rounds.

TO MAKE A SOLID MANDALA

Work as for a duo-tone mandala, using a size D-3 (3.25 mm) hook and omitting Round 9, working Round 10 into ch-4 sp of Round 8. There is no need to fasten off the yarn after Rounds 4 and 6 but instead, slip stitch into the nearest space where the next color may have been attached—if you are not already there.

Feel-good tip

When your crochet is finished, why not carry your calming mandala around with you? Use it as a touchstone during moments of stress or anxiety. Touch it, immerse yourself in the calming colors, and recall that feeling of being in the center of calm. Let the gentle concentric ripples fill your world.

Comforting Pillow

This pillow emulates the calming ripples of water. Use your favorite colors for a more personal look. Crocheted in the round, with three-dimensional ripples made as you go, this pattern is perfect for the confident novice.

YOU WILL NEED

* Super bulky-weight, acrylic/wool blend yarn (approx. 6 oz/170 g; 106 yds/97 m)
  MC 2 balls in navy
  CCa 1 ball in glacier
  CCb 1 ball in sky blue
  CCc 1 ball in denim
* 5 buttons, to fit loops (approx. 1¼"/28 mm)
* Circular pillow form, 16" (40 cm)
* Size M/N-13 (9 mm) hook
* Yarn needle

GAUGE

9 dc and 4 rounds measure 4" (10 cm).

DIMENSIONS

15" (38 cm) in diameter before seaming.
To fit a 16" (40 cm) circular pillow form.

NOTE

The front of the pillow has rounds of tucks, which are worked over two rounds and are made of folded treble stitches. On Rounds 3, 6, and 9, treble stitches are worked into the front loop only (flo) of the stitches on the preceding round. On the second round (tuck round), stitches are worked into the treble stitches and the un-worked back loop (blo) of the stitches on the round preceding the round of treble stitches.

TO MAKE THE BACK PANEL OF THE PILLOW

Using MC, ch4, sl st into fourth ch from hook to form a ring.

Round 1: ch3 (counts as first dc), 11dc into ring, sl st into top of beg ch-3 to join. (12 sts)

Round 2: ch3 (counts as first dc), 1dc into base of beg ch-3, 2dc into each st to end of round, sl st into top of beg ch-3 to join. (24 sts)

Round 3: ch3 (counts as first dc), 2dc into next st, [1dc into next st, 2dc into next st] 11 times, sl st into top of beg ch-3 to join. (36 sts)

Round 4: ch3 (counts as first dc), 1dc into next st, 2dc into next st, [1dc into each of next 2 sts, 2dc into next st] 11 times, sl st into top of beg ch-3 to join. (48 sts)

Round 5: ch3 (counts as first dc), 1dc into each of next 2 sts, 2dc into next st, [1dc into each of next 3 sts, 2dc into next st] 11 times, sl st into top of beg ch-3 to join. (60 sts)

Round 6: ch3 (counts as first dc), 1dc into each of next 3 sts, 2dc into next st, [1dc into each of next 4 sts, 2dc into next st] 11 times, sl st into top of beg ch-3 to join. (72 sts)

Round 7: ch3 (counts as first dc), 1dc into each of next 4 sts, 2dc into next st, [1dc into each of next 5 sts, 2dc into next st] 11 times, sl st into top of beg ch-3 to join. (84 sts)

Round 8: ch3 (counts as first dc), 1dc into each of next 5 sts, 2dc into next st, [1dc into each of next 6 sts, 2dc into next st] 11 times, sl st into top of beg ch-3 to join. (96 sts)
Fasten off.

TO MAKE THE FRONT PANEL OF THE PILLOW

Using MC, ch 4, sl st into fourth ch from hook to form a ring.

Round 1: ch3 (counts as first dc), 11dc into ring, sl st into top of beg ch-3 to join. (12 sts)

Round 2: ch3 (counts as first dc), 1dc into base of beg of ch-3, 2dc into each st to end of round, do not fasten off MC, join in CCa, sl st into flo of top of beg ch-3 to join. (24 sts)

Round 3: using CCa, ch4 (counts as first tr), 1tr flo into each st to end of round, fasten off CCa leaving an 8" (20 cm) tail, using MC, sl st at the same time into both top of beg ch-4 and blo of beg ch-3 of previous round to join. (24 sts)

Round 4 (tuck): ch3 (counts as first dc), working at the same time into both the st indicated on Round 3 and blo of corresponding st of Round 2, folding tr sts as you work, 2dc into both next sts, [1dc into both next sts, 2dc into both next sts] to last st, sl st into top of beg ch-3 to join. (36 sts)

Round 5: ch3 (counts as first dc), 1dc into next st, 2dc into next st, [1dc into each of next 2 sts, 2dc into next st] 11 times, do not fasten off MC, join in CCb with sl st into flo of top of beg ch-3 to join. (48 dc)

Round 6: using CCb instead of CCa, repeat Round 3. (48 tr)

Round 7 (tuck): ch3 (counts as first dc), working at the same time into both the st indicated on Round 6 and blo of corresponding st of Round 5, folding tr sts as you work, 1dc into each of next 2 sts, 2dc into next st, [1dc into each of next 3 sts, 2dc into next st] to last st, sl st into top of beg ch-3 to join. (60 sts)

Round 8: ch3 (counts as first dc), 1dc into each of next 3 sts, 2dc into next st, [1dc into each of next 4 sts, 2dc into next st] 11 times, do not fasten off MC, join in CCc with sl st into flo of top of beg ch-3 to join. (72 sts)

Round 9: using CCc instead of CCa, repeat Round 3. (72 sts)

Round 10 (tuck): ch3 (counts as first dc), working at the same time into both the st indicated on Round 9 and blo of corresponding st of Round 8, folding tr sts as you work, 1dc into each of next 4 sts, 2dc into next st, [1dc into each of next 5 sts, 2dc into next st] to last st, sl st into top of beg ch-3 to join. (84 sts)

Round 11: ch3 (counts as first dc), 1dc into each of next 5 sts, 2dc into next st, [1dc into each of next 6 sts, 2dc into next st] 11 times, sl st into top of beg ch-3 to join. (96 sts)
Place the wrong sides of the front and back panels together.

Round 12: ch1, working at the same time into the sts indicated on both the front and back panels, 1 rev sc into each of the next 76 sts, working into the front panel only, 1 rev sc flo into each of the next 20 sts, without turning the work, working back along the sts just worked, ch 1, working into the un-worked back loops, 1sc into each of next 2 sts, 1hdc into each of next 2 sts, 1dc into each of next 12 sts, 1hdc into each of next 2 sts, 1sc into each of next 2 sts, turn. (20 sts)

Button loop row: ch1, 1sc into each of next 2 sts, [ch3, 1sc into each of next 4 sts] 4 times, ch3, 1sc into each of next 2 sts. Fasten off.

FINISHING

Weave in loose ends. Sew the buttons onto the back panel, opposite button loops along Round 7. The two buttons on either end may need to be a little closer to Round 8, to accommodate the slight curve of the button-loop flap.

Feel-good tip

Use this tactile pillow as a comfort in moments of stress. Trace your fingers around the concentric circles to remind yourself of the calming ripples of your meditation. Gently rediscover that place of calm in your mind.

Energy

Do this exercise anytime you need to find energy or motivation. Practicing it with your eyes open and then closed will enable you to use it any time, anywhere—even at your desk when that dreaded mid-afternoon energy slump strikes.

1 Sit comfortably upright with both feet on the ground. Allow yourself to feel supported by your chair, and be aware of your feet equally on the floor.

2 Bring the focus of your attention to a central spot situated a couple of inches below the lower tip of your breastbone.

3 Intensify your focus on this area and imagine it as your source of vital energy—a life-force full of warmth coming from your very core.

4 Breathe deeply into the depths of your lungs and feel this core get warmer and more energized with each breath you take. Focus on your breath and the essential life it brings.

5 Feel a sense of vitality radiating outward from this core, filling your body with a zest for life.

6 Become aware of this energy coursing through your body to the very tip of your fingertips and toes. Feel them tingle with awareness.

7 Feel the energy light up your brain, your thoughts, and your ideas, and take a moment to dwell on the sensation of being vibrantly alive.

8 As the energy fills your body and mind, it extends outward to fill the space around you, surrounding you with an aura of vitality and positivity that others will sense and respond to. You feel full of creative power and potential. Feel the sensation empowering you. Feel vibrantly alive.

9 Bask in the glow of this sensation for a moment. Repeat as often as necessary to feel truly energized.

Radiating Mandalas

These mandalas begin with warmth in the center that radiates out. The lovely shell stitches leave room for a burst of the colorful wool felt backing to shine through.

YOU WILL NEED

* DK-weight, wool yarn (approx. 3½ oz/100 g; 306 yds/280 m)
  CCa 1 ball in bright pink
  CCb 1 ball in orange
  CCc 1 ball in mustard
  CCd 1 ball in yellow
  CCe 1 ball in white

* Wool felt sheets, 8" (20 cm) square, 1 sheet of each: hot pink; light pink; yellow.

* Size G-6 (4 mm) hook

* Yarn needle

* Sewing needle and matching sewing thread

GAUGE

Simple and blossoming mandalas: Rounds 1–4 measure 3¼" (8 cm) in diameter.

Intricate mandala: Rounds 1–4 measure 2¾" (7 cm) in diameter.

DIMENSIONS

Simple mandala: 6¼" (16 cm) in diameter.

Blossoming mandala: 7" (18 cm) in diameter.

Intricate mandala: 7" (18 cm) in diameter.

TO MAKE THE SIMPLE MANDALA

Using CCb, make a magic ring.

Round 1: ch3 (counts as first dc), 11dc into ring, sl st into top of beg ch-3 to join. (12 sts)

Round 2: ch3 (counts as first dc), 1dc into base of beg ch-3, 2dc into each st to end of round. (24 sts)

Fasten off and make an invisible join.

Join in CCa into any st.

Round 3: ch3 (counts as first dc), 1dc into base of beg ch-3, [1dc into next st, 2dc into next st,] 11 times, 1dc into next st, sl st into top of beg ch-3 to join. (36 sts)

Round 4: ch3 (counts as first dc), 1dc into base of beg ch-3, [1dc into each of next 2 sts, 2dc into next st] 11 times, 1dc into each of next 2 sts. (48 sts)

Fasten off and make an invisible join.

Join in CCd into any st.

Round 5: ch3 (counts as first dc), 4dc into base of beg ch-3, skip 3 sts, [5dc into next st, skip 3 sts] 11 times.

(60 sts—12 shells/5-dc groups)

Fasten off and make an invisible join.

Join in CCe into any sp between two shells.

Round 6: ch3 (counts as first dc), 1dc into base of beg ch-3, 1dc into each of next 4 sts, [2dc into next sp, 1dc into each of next 4 sts] 11 times. (72 sts)

Fasten off and make an invisible join.

Join in CCb into any st.

Round 7: ch2 (counts as first hdc), 1hdc into base of beg ch-2, 1hdc into each of next 5 sts, [2hdc into next st, 1hdc into each of next 5 sts] 11 times. (84 sts)

Fasten off and make an invisible join.

Join in CCa into any st.

Round 8: ch2 (counts as first hdc), 1hdc into base of beg ch-2, 1hdc into each of next 6 sts, [2hdc into next st, 1hdc into each of next 6 sts] 11 times. (96 sts)

Fasten off and make an invisible join.

Join in CCd into any st.

Round 9: ch1, 1sc into next st, ch5, sl st into base of last sc, [1sc into each of next 3 sts, ch5, sl st into base of last sc] 31 times, 1sc into next st.

Fasten off and make an invisible join.

TO MAKE THE BLOSSOMING MANDALA

Using CCa, make a magic ring.

Round 1: ch3 (counts as first dc), 11dc into ring. (12 sts)

Fasten off and make an invisible join.

Join in CCb into any st.

Round 2: ch3 (counts as first dc), 1dc into base of beg ch-3, 2dc into each st to end of round. (24 sts)

Fasten off and make an invisible join.

Join in CCc into any st.

Round 3: ch3 (counts as first dc), 1dc into base of beg ch-3, [1dc into next st, 2dc into next st] 11 times, 1dc into next st. (36 sts)

Fasten off and make an invisible join.

Join in CCd into any st.

Round 4: ch3 (counts as first dc), 1dc into base of beg ch-3, [1dc into each of next 2 sts, 2dc into next st] 11 times, 1dc into each of next 2 sts. (48 sts)

Fasten off and make an invisible join.

Join in CCe into any st.

Round 5: ch3 (counts as first dc), 4dc into base of beg ch-3, skip 3 sts, [5dc into next st, skip 3 sts] 11 times.

(60 sts—12 shells/5-dc groups)

Fasten off and make an invisible join.

Join in CCa into any sp between two shells.

Round 6: ch3 (counts as first dc), 1dc into base of beg ch-3, 1dc into each of next 4 sts, [2dc into next sp, 1dc into each of next 4 sts] 11 times. (72 sts)

Fasten off and make an invisible join.

Join in CCb into any st.

Round 7: ch3 (counts as first dc), 1dc into base of beg ch-3, 1dc into each of next 5 sts, [2dc into next st, 1dc into each of next 5 sts] 11 times. (84 sts)

Fasten off and make an invisible join.

Join in CCc into any st.

Round 8: ch1, 1sc into base of beg ch-1, 1sc into each of next 6 sts, [2sc into next st, 1sc into each of next 6 sts] 11 times. (96 sts)

Fasten off and make an invisible join.

Join in CCd into sc directly above any sp between two shells on Round 5.

Round 9: ch3 (counts as first dc), 6dc into base of beg ch-3, ch2, skip 7 sts, [7dc into next st, ch2, skip 7 sts] 11 times. (108 sts)

Fasten off and make an invisible join.

Join in CCe into any ch-2 sp.

Round 10: ch3 (counts as first dc), 3dc into ch-2 sp at base of beg ch-3, 1dc into each of next 6 sts (over shell), [4dc into next ch-2 sp, 1dc into each of next 6 sts (over shell)] 11 times. (120 sts)

Fasten off and make an invisible join.

TO MAKE THE INTRICATE MANDALA

Using CCb, make a magic ring.

Round 1: ch3 (counts as first dc), 11dc into ring. (12 sts)

OPPOSITE From top: simple mandala, blossoming mandala, and intricate mandala.

Fasten off and make an invisible join.

Join in CCa into any st.

Round 2: ch3 (counts as first dc), 1dc into base of beg ch-3, 2dc into each st to end of round. (24 sts)

Fasten off and make an invisible join.

Join in CCd into any st.

Round 3: ch2 (counts as first hdc), 1hdc into base of beg ch-2, [1hdc into next st, 2hdc into next st] 11 times, 1hdc into next st. (36 sts)

Fasten off and make an invisible join.

Join in CCe into any st.

Round 4: ch2 (counts as first hdc), 1hdc into base of beg ch-2, [1hdc into each of next 2 sts, 2hdc into next st] 11 times, 1hdc into each of next 2 sts. (48 sts)

Fasten off and make an invisible join.

Join in CCb into any st.

Round 5: ch3 (counts as first dc), 4dc into base of beg ch-3, skip 3 sts, [5dc into next st, skip 3 sts] 11 times. (60 sts—12 shells/5-dc groups)

Fasten off and make an invisible join.

Join in CCc into any sp between two shells.

Round 6: ch3 (counts as first dc), 1dc into base of beg ch-3, 1dc into each of next 4 sts, [2dc into next sp, 1dc into each of next 4 sts] 11 times. (72 sts)

Fasten off and make an invisible join.

Join in CCe into any st.

Round 7: ch1 (counts as first sc), 1sc into base of beg ch-1, 1sc into each of next 5 sts, [2sc into next st, 1sc into each of next 5 sts] 11 times. (84 sts)

Fasten off and make an invisible join. Join in CCa into sc directly above any sp between two shells on Round 5.

Round 8: ch3 (counts as first dc), 7dc into base of beg ch-3, skip 6 sts, [8dc into next st, skip 6 sts] 11 times.
(96 sts—12 shells/8-dc groups)
Fasten off and make an invisible join.
Join in CCd into any sp between two shells on Round 8.

Round 9: ch3 (counts as first dc), 1dc into sp at base of beg ch-3, 1dc into each of next 7 sts (over shell), [2dc into sp between shells, 1dc into each of next 7 sts] 11 times. (108 sts)
Fasten off and make an invisible join.
Join in CCc into dc at top of any point.

Round 10: ch3 (counts as first dc), 1dc into base of beg ch-3, 1dc into each of next 7 sts, [2dc into next st, 1dc into each of next 8 sts] 11 times. (120 sts)
Fasten off and make an invisible join.

FINISHING

Block mandalas to finished dimensions.
Weave in loose ends.

Simple mandala

Cut a 6" (15 cm) diameter circle from the light pink wool felt and using matching thread and blanket stitch, sew to the back of the mandala.

Blossoming mandala

Cut a 6½" (16.5 cm) diameter circle from the hot pink wool felt and using matching thread and blanket stitch, sew to the back of the mandala.

Intricate mandala

Cut a 6½" (14.5 cm) diameter circle from the yellow felt and using matching thread and blanket stitch, sew to the back of the mandala.

Feel-good tip

We all need a boost of energy from time to time—carry your mandalas with you and use them as a portable pick-me-up. Experience their tactile energy and immerse yourself totally in the vibrancy of their colors. As you do so, recall the energizing exercise whenever and wherever you need a zestful lift.

Sun Salutation Yoga Mat Bag

Salute the day with this vibrantly colored bag made to carry your yoga mat.
Feel the warmth of the sun rising while working on each radiating mandala.

YOU WILL NEED

* DK-weight, wool yarn (approx. 3½ oz/100 g; 306 yds/280 m)
  CCa 1 ball in yellow
  CCb 1 ball in orange
  CCc 1 ball in bright pink
  CCd 1 ball in teal
  CCe 1 ball in dark blue

* Robert Kaufman, Kona Cotton, 2 yds (2 m) of 44" (112 cm) wide fabric, in canary.

* Size G-6 (4 mm) hook

* Yarn needle

* Dressmaker's pins

* Fabric glue

* Sewing thread in matching navy blue and yellow

* Sewing needle

* Sewing machine

* Fusible web or fusible adhesive to match fabric weight and used for sewing (optional)

* Clothes iron

* Serger (optional)

GAUGE

Rounds 1–4 measure 3" (7.5 cm) diameter.

DIMENSIONS

Base mandala: 6½" (16 cm) in diameter.
Side mandalas: 7¼" (18.5 cm) in diameter.
Yoga bag width (laid flat): 11½" (29 cm).
Yoga bag height: 31" (79 cm).

SPECIAL STITCHES

spike-2: spike stitch 2 rows below— skip next st but work corresponding stitch 2 rows below.

spike-3: spike stitch 3 rows below— skip next st but work corresponding stitch 3 rows below.

spike-4: spike stitch 4 rows below— skip next st but work corresponding stitch 4 rows below.

TO MAKE THE TOP ROW MANDALAS (MAKE THREE)

Using CCa, make a magic ring.

Round 1: ch3 (counts as first dc), 11dc into the ring. (12 sts)

Fasten off and make an invisible join.

Join in CCa into any st.

Round 2: ch3 (counts as first dc), 1dc into base of beg ch-3, 2dc into each st to end of round. (24 sts)

Fasten off and make an invisible join.

Join in CCa into any st.

Round 3: ch3 (counts as first dc), 1dc into base of beg ch-3, [1dc into next st, 2dc into next st] 11 times, 1dc into next st. (36 sts)

Fasten off and make an invisible join.

Join in CCa into any st.

Round 4: ch3 (counts as first dc), 1dc into base of beg ch-3, [1dc into each of next 2 sts, 2dc into next st] 11 times, 1dc into each of next 2 sts. (48 sts)

Fasten off and make an invisible join.

Join in CCa into any st.

Round 5: ch3 (counts as first dc), 1dc into base of beg ch-3, [1dc into each of next 3 sts, 2dc into next st] 11 times, 1dc into each of next 3 sts. (60 sts)

Fasten off and make an invisible join.

Join in CCa into any st.

Round 6: ch3 (counts as first dc), 1dc into base of beg ch-3, [1dc into each of next 4 sts, 2dc into next st] 11 times, 1dc into each of next 4 sts. (72 sts)

Fasten off and make an invisible join.

Join in CCb into any st.

Round 7: ch3 (counts as first dc), 1dc into base of beg ch–3, 1dc into each of next 2 sts, 1dc spike-4, 1dc into each of next 2 sts, [2dc into next st, 1dc into each of next 2 sts, 1dc spike-4, 1dc into each of next 2 sts] 11 times. (84 sts)

Fasten off and make an invisible join.

Join in CCc into any st above a spike-4.

Round 8: ch3 (counts as first dc), 1dc into base of beg ch–3, 1dc into each of next 3 sts, 1dc spike-2, 1dc into each of next 2 sts, [2dc into next st, 1dc into each of next 3 sts, 1dc spike-2, 1dc into each of next 2 sts] 11 times. (96 sts)

Fasten off and make an invisible join.

Join in CCd into any st.

Round 9: ch3 (counts as first dc), 1dc into base of beg ch–3, [1dc into each of next 7 sts, 2dc into next st] 11 times, 1dc into each of next 7 sts. (108 sts)

Fasten off and make an invisible join.

Join in CCe into any st.

Round 10: ch3 (counts as first dc), 1dc into base of beg ch–3, [1dc into each of next 8 sts, 2dc into next st] 11 times, 1dc into each of next 8 sts. (120 sts)

Fasten off and make an invisible join.

TO MAKE THE SECOND ROW MANDALAS (MAKE THREE)

Using CCa, make a magic ring.

Rounds 1–5: work as the top row mandala.

Fasten off and make an invisible join.

Join in CCb into any st.

Round 6: ch3 (counts as first dc), 1dc into base of beg ch–3, 1dc into next st, 1dc spike-3, 1dc into each of next 2 sts, [2dc into next st, 1dc into next st, 1dc spike-3, 1dc into each of next 2 sts] 11 times. (72 sts)

Fasten off and make an invisible join.

Join in CCb into any st.

Round 7: ch3 (counts as first dc), 1dc into base of beg ch–3, [1dc into each of next 5 sts, 2dc into next st] 11 times, 1dc into each of next 5 sts. (84 sts)

Fasten off and make an invisible join.

Join in CCc into any st above a spike-3.

Round 8: ch3 (counts as first dc), 1dc into base of beg ch–3, 1dc into each of next 3 sts, 1dc spike-2, 1dc into each of next 2 sts, [2dc into next st, 1dc into each of next 3 sts, 1dc spike-2, 1dc into each of next 2 sts] 11 times. (96 sts)

Fasten off and make an invisible join.

Join in CCd into any st.

Round 9: ch3 (counts as first dc), 1dc into base of beg ch–3, [1dc into each of next 7 sts, 2dc into next st] 11 times, 1dc into each of next 7 sts. (108 sts)

Fasten off and make an invisible join.

Join in CCe into any st.

Round 10: ch3 (counts as first dc), 1dc into base of beg ch-3, [1dc into each of next 8 sts, 2dc into next st] 11 times, 1dc into each of next 8 sts. (120 sts)

Fasten off and make an invisible join.

TO MAKE THE THIRD ROW MANDALAS (MAKE THREE)

Using CCa, make a magic ring.

Rounds 1–4: work as the top row mandala.

Fasten off and make an invisible join.

Join in CCb into any st.

Round 5: ch3 (counts as first dc), 1dc into base of beg ch-3, 1dc into next st, 1dc spike-2, 1dc into next st, [2dc into next st, 1dc into next st, 1dc spike-2, 1dc into next st] 11 times. (60 sts)

Fasten off and make an invisible join.

Join in CCb into any st.

Round 6: ch3 (counts as first dc), 1dc into base of beg ch-3, [1dc into each of next 4 sts, 2dc into next st] 11 times, 1dc into each of next 4 sts. (72 sts)

Fasten off and make an invisible join.

Join in CCc into any st above a spike-2.

When working spike stitches, take care to draw the strand worked into the stitch up to the height of the previous stitch before completing the stitch.

Round 7: ch 3, 1dc into base of beg ch-3, 1dc into each of next 2 sts, 1dc spike-2, 1dc into each of next 2 sts, [2dc into next st, 1dc into each of next 2 sts, 1dc spike-2, 1dc into each of next 2 sts] 11 times. (84 sts)

Fasten off and make an invisible join.

Join in CCc into any st.

Round 8: ch3 (counts as first dc), 1dc into base of beg ch-3, [1dc into each of next 6 sts, 2dc into next st] 11 times, 1dc into each of next 6 sts. (96 sts)

Fasten off and make an invisible join.

Join in CCd into any st.

Round 9: ch3 (counts as first dc), 1dc into base of beg ch-3, [1dc into each of next 7 sts, 2dc into next st] 11 times, 1dc into each of next 7 sts. (108 sts)

Fasten off and make an invisible join.

Join in CCe into any st.

Round 10: ch3 (counts as first dc), 1dc into base of beg ch-3, [1dc into each of next 8 sts,

2dc into next st] 11 times, 1dc into each of next 8 sts. (120 sts)

Fasten off and make an invisible join.

TO MAKE THE LOWER ROW MANDALAS (MAKE THREE)

Using CCa, make a magic ring.

Rounds 1–3: work as the top row mandala. Fasten off and make an invisible join. Join in CCb into any st.

Rounds 4–5: using CCb, work as the top row mandala. Fasten off and make an invisible join. Join in CCc into any st.

Round 6: using CCc, work as the top row mandala. Fasten off and make an invisible join. Join in CCc into any st.

Round 7: ch3 (counts as first dc), 1dc into base of beg ch-3, [1dc into each of next 5 sts, 2dc into next st] 11 times, 1dc into each of next 5 sts. (84 sts)

Fasten off and make an invisible join. Join in CCd into any st.

Round 8: ch3 (counts as first dc), 1dc into base of beg ch-3, [1dc into each of next 6 sts, 2dc into next st] 11 times, 1dc into each of next 6 sts. (96 sts)

Fasten off and make an invisible join. Join in CCd into any st.

Round 9: ch3 (counts as first dc), 1dc into base of beg ch-3, [1dc into each of next 7 sts, 2dc into next st] 11 times, 1dc into each of next 7 sts. (108 sts)

Fasten off and make an invisible join. Join in CCe into any st.

Round 10: ch3 (counts as first dc), 1dc into base of beg ch-3, [1dc into each of next 8 sts, 2dc into next st] 11 times, 1dc into each of next 8 sts. (120 sts)

Fasten off and make an invisible join.

TO MAKE THE BASE MANDALA (MAKE ONE)

Using CCa, make a magic ring.

Rounds 1–2: work as the top row mandala. Fasten off and make an invisible join. Join in CCb into any st.

Rounds 3–4: using CCb, work as the top row mandala. Fasten off and make an invisible join. Join in CCc into any st.

Rounds 5–6: using CCb, work as the top row mandala. Fasten off and make an invisible join. Join in CCd into any st.

Round 7: ch3 (counts as first dc), 1dc into base of beg ch-3, [1dc into each of next 5 sts, 2dc into next st] 11 times, 1dc into each of next 5 sts. (84 sts)

Fasten off and make an invisible join. Join in CCd into any st.

Round 8: ch3 (counts as first dc), 1dc into base of beg ch-3, [1dc into each of next 6 sts, 2dc into next st] 11 times, 1dc into each of next 6 sts. (96 sts)

Fasten off and make an invisible join. Join in CCe into any st.

Tip

For a stronger strap, replace double crochet with single crochet—on Row 1, work the first stitch into the second chain from hook.

Round 9: ch3 (counts as first dc), 1dc into base of beg ch-3, [1dc into each of next 7 sts, 2dc into next st] 11 times, 1dc into each of next 7 sts. (108 sts)
Fasten off and make an invisible join.

TO MAKE THE DRAWSTRING BAND

Using CCe, ch122.
Row 1: 1dc into fourth ch from the hook (counts as first and second dc), 1dc into each ch to end, turn. (120 sts)
Row 2: ch3 (counts as first dc), 1dc into each of next 4 sts, ch1, skip 1 st, [1dc into each of next 9 sts, ch1, skip 1 st] 11 times, 1dc into each of next 4 sts, turn.
Row 3: ch3 (counts as first dc), 1dc into each st and ch-1 sp to end of row, turn. (120 sts)
Row 4: ch3 (counts as first dc), 1dc into each st to end of row.
Fasten off. Whip stitch short ends together to form the drawstring band. Weave in loose ends.

TO MAKE THE DRAWSTRING

Using CCd, ch until piece measures 40" (102 cm). Fasten off.

TO MAKE THE SHOULDER STRAP

Using CCe, loosely ch172.
Row 1: 1dc into fourth ch from hook (counts as first and second dc), 1dc into each ch to end, turn. (170 sts)
Rows 2–5: ch3 (counts as first dc), 1dc into each st to end, turn.
Fasten off. Weave in loose ends.

FINISHING

Prewash and iron the cotton fabric. From the fabric, cut two 24 × 30" (60 × 76 cm) rectangles, and two 7" (18 cm) diameter circles. Block the base mandala to 6½" (16.5 cm) diameter, and the side mandalas to 7¼" (18.5 cm) diameter.

Using the photographs on pages 41 and 44 as reference, on a flat surface, place one 24 × 30" (60 × 76 cm) rectangle of fabric and lay out the side mandalas in row order. Center the mandalas so that the lower row mandalas are ¼" (6 mm) from the lower edge, the top row mandalas are ¾" (18 mm) from the top edge, and all the mandalas are ½" (12 mm) from the side edges. Pin the mandalas in place, and using CCe, whip stitch the mandalas together at the points where the mandalas meet.

Using navy blue thread, either hand or machine stitch the mandalas to the fabric. Fusible web or fusible adhesive may be used to attach the mandalas in place instead of straight pins. This is especially helpful if you are machine sewing.

Fold the rectangle with the mandalas, right sides together, in half lengthwise. Using the yellow thread, sew along the 30" (76 cm) edge leaving a ½" (12 mm) seam allowance. Pin one 7" (18 cm) diameter fabric circle to the bottom edge of the bag by the lower row mandalas. Using yellow thread, sew leaving a ¼" (6 mm) seam allowance.

Turn bag right-side out, and pin and hand stitch the base mandala to the base of the bag. Using CCe, whip stitch the mandalas together at the points where the mandalas meet.

To make the lining

Fold the remaining 24 × 30" (60 × 76 cm) rectangle, right sides together, in half lengthwise. Using the yellow thread, sew along the 30" (76 cm) edge leaving a ½" (12 mm) seam allowance. Pin the remaining 7" (18 cm) diameter fabric circle to the bottom edge. Using yellow thread, sew leaving a ¼" (6 mm) seam allowance.

To assemble the bag

Fold the top edge of both bag tops over by ¼" (6 mm) to the wrong side, and press.

Serge or zigzag stitch all sewn seam allowances. Put the lining inside the bag with the wrong sides together. Align the top edges and pin the drawstring band onto the outside with Row 4 touching the top of the top row mandalas, and pin in place. Be sure that the little holes for the drawstring are not overlapping the fabric. Sew the band and lining in place with matching thread. Stitch one short-edge of the strap to the base of the bag, on the last round of the base mandala, and the other end to the bottom of the band.

Thread the drawstring through the band's holes and tie a knot in the ends to finish. Seal the ends of the drawstring with a drop of fabric glue.

Feel-good tip

Use a reviving yoga session to stimulate the flow of energy around your whole body. Keep your sun salutation bag near your mat to help focus your mind on your intentions to bring vibrancy, vitality, and motivation to your practice.

Relax

Where possible, practice this visualization exercise outside. Take off your shoes and socks, and sit comfortably on a seat or stool with both feet on the ground.

1 Close your eyes. Focus your thoughts on the sensations coming from the soles of your feet. Feel the connection with the ground or floor beneath them and notice its temperature and texture.

2 Now imagine you are on a beach—perhaps it's your favorite beach or an imaginary sandy shoreline stretching before you. The sand is warm beneath your feet.

3 Become aware of the sand's graininess between your toes as it gently brushes over your feet in the light, warm breeze.

4 In the distance you can hear the sea. It's a gentle, calm day so the waves are lapping the shoreline rhythmically. The sun is warm enough to relax you but not too hot— everything is just right.

5 Feel a light sea breeze kiss your cheeks and ripple through your hair. It brings with it the sound of distant, happy laughter and seagulls soaring high above. These sounds mingle with the sound of the waves.

6 Visualize yourself walking along the shoreline, and as you do so, notice the pebbles and shells washed up by the sea. Feel inspired by their colors and textures.

7 Notice a piece of weathered wood entangled in seaweed and the odd bright smattering of flotsam discarded by the tide.

8 Feel refreshed by the sea air and motivated by the colors and textures of the shoreline.

9 Open your eyes and observe your surroundings just like a newcomer exploring the colors and textures of a fresh seashore.

Wave Wrap

Inspired by the sea, this wrap was designed to promote relaxation. The pattern repeats are meditative and calming, and the colors encourage serenity and peace of mind.

YOU WILL NEED

* DK-weight, wool/acrylic/cashmere blend yarns (approx. 1¾ oz/50 g; 137 yds/125 m)
CCa 2 balls in dark gray
CCb 1 ball in indigo
CCc 1 ball in denim
CCd 1 ball in teal
CCe 1 ball in mist
CCf 1 ball in light blue
CCg 1 ball in slate
CCh 1 ball in cream
* Size I-9 (5.5 mm) hook
* Size H-8 (5 mm) hook
* Yarn needle

GAUGE

3 shells (18 sts) measure 4" (10 cm) and 6 shells (12 rows) measure 4¼" (10.5 cm) over pattern, using size H-8 (5 mm) hook.

DIMENSIONS

65" (165 cm) long and 18" (46 cm) wide across the widest part.

NOTES

* Each 5-dc group counts as one shell.
* This wrap is worked from the top down. Each row will have one less shell than the previous row, creating a triangular piece.
* You will need a multiple of 6 plus 2 chains to start. If you would like to make a larger wrap, simply add multiples of 6 chains. Remember that the wrap is triangular, so adding repeats will automatically add rows as well.

TO MAKE THE WAVE WRAP

Using size I-9 (5.5 mm) hook and CCa, ch302 (50 repeats of 6 plus 2).
Change to size H-8 (5 mm) hook.

Row 1: working into the back bumps, sl st into second ch from hook, [skip 2 ch, 5dc into next ch, skip 2 ch, 1sc into next ch] rep until 6 ch remain, skip 2 ch, 5dc into next ch, skip 2 ch, sl st into last ch, turn.

Row 2: skip sl st, sl st into each of next 3 dc, [skip 2 dc, 5dc into next sc, skip 2 dc, 1sc into next dc] rep until 8 sts remain, skip 2 dc, 5dc into next sc, skip 2 dc, sl st into next dc, leaving 2 sts unworked, turn.

Rows 3–6: repeat Row 2.

Row 7: skip sl st, sl st into each of next 2 dc, fasten off CCa, join in CCb into next dc with a sl st, [skip 2 dc, 5dc into next sc, skip 2 dc, 1sc into next dc] rep until 8 sts remain, skip 2 dc, 5dc into next sc, skip 2 dc, sl st into next dc, leaving 2 sts unworked, turn.

Rows 8–12: repeat Row 2.

Row 13: skip sl st, sl st into each of next 2 dc, fasten off CCb, join in CCc into next dc with a sl st, [skip 2 dc, 5dc into next sc, skip 2 dc, 1sc into next dc] rep until 8 sts remain, skip 2 dc, 5dc into next sc, skip 2 dc, sl st into next dc, leaving 2 sts unworked, turn.

Rows 14–18: repeat Row 2.

Row 19: skip sl st, sl st into each of next 2 dc, fasten off CCc, join in CCd into next dc with a sl st, [skip 2 dc, 5dc into next sc, skip 2 dc, 1sc into next dc] rep until 8 sts remain, skip 2 dc, 5dc into next sc, skip 2 dc, sl st into next dc, leaving 2 sts unworked, turn.

Rows 20–24: repeat Row 2.

Row 25: skip sl st, sl st into each of next 2 dc, fasten off CCd, join in CCe into next dc with a sl st, [skip 2 dc, 5dc into next sc, skip 2 dc, 1sc into next dc] rep until 8 sts remain, skip 2 dc,

5dc into next sc, skip 2 dc, sl st into next dc, leaving 2 sts unworked, turn.

Rows 26–30: repeat Row 2.

Row 31: skip sl st, sl st into each of next 2 dc, fasten off CCe, join in CCf into next dc with a sl st, [skip 2 dc, 5dc into next sc, skip 2 dc, 1sc into next dc] rep until 8 sts remain, skip 2 dc, 5dc into next sc, skip 2 dc, sl st into next dc, leaving 2 sts unworked, turn.

Rows 32–36: repeat Row 2.

Row 37: skip sl st, sl st into each of next 2 dc, fasten off CCf, join in CCg into next dc with a sl st, [skip 2 dc, 5dc into next sc, skip 2 dc, 1sc into next dc] rep until 8 sts remain, skip 2 dc, 5dc into next sc, skip 2 dc, sl st into next dc, leaving 2 sts unworked, turn.

Rows 38–42: repeat Row 2.

Row 43: skip sl st, sl st into each of next 2 dc, fasten off CCg, join in CCh into next dc with a sl st, [skip 2 dc, 5dc into next sc, skip 2 dc, 1sc into next dc] rep until 8 sts remain, skip 2 dc,

5dc into next sc, skip 2 dc, sl st into next dc, leaving 2 sts unworked, turn.

Rows 44–48: repeat Row 2.

Row 49: skip sl st, sl st into each of next 3 dc, skip 2 dc, 5dc into next sc, skip 2 dc, 1sc into next dc, skip 2 dc, 5dc into next sc, skip 2 dc, sl st into next dc, leaving 2 sts unworked, turn.

Row 50: skip sl st, sl st into each of next 3 dc, skip 2 dc, 5dc into next sc, skip 2 dc, sl st into next dc.

Fasten off.

FINISHING

To block the wrap, pin it out onto a padded surface, taking care not to overstretch the stitches, and to pin it out symmetrically. Spray the wrap lightly with cool water. Allow the wrap to dry before removing the pins.

Weave in loose ends.

Feel-good tip

Imagine the repeating sound of the ocean as you rhythmically crochet the shells of your pattern. Use your wave wrap to keep you warm outdoors and remind yourself to be mindfully aware of nature's incredible array of textures and colors.

Meditation Seat Pillow

Recreate your own personal beach space with this large floor pillow. The pattern is easy and soothing to make, and the resulting pillow is perfect for using during meditation, either indoors or outside.

YOU WILL NEED

* Worsted-weight, acrylic/wool blend yarn (approx. 3 oz/85g; 197 yds/180m) in 3 balls in cream
* Sturdy upholstery fabric in a similar shade to the yarn, 24 x 55" (60 x 140 cm) or a fabric pillow cover to fit your pillow form
* Square pillow form 22" (56 cm)
* Size L-11 (8 mm) hook
* Size M/N-13 (9 mm) hook
* Stitch markers, 4
* Yarn needle
* Sewing machine
* Sewing needle and matching thread
* Dressmaker's pins

GAUGE

39 sts measure 4" (10 cm) and 6 rows measure 4¾" (12 cm) over pattern.

DIMENSIONS

22" (56 cm) square—before seaming.

NOTES

• The crochet fabric in this pattern is quite stretchy. If the finished panel is a bit short of the required size, just pull the crochet fabric gently and measure it again. To make the pillow cover larger, work more edging rounds.
• Instead of making a pillow cover, you can buy a 22" (56 cm) square pillow cover in a similar shade to the yarn.

TO MAKE THE PILLOW PANEL

Using size L-11 (8 mm) hook, ch43.

Row 1: 1hdc into second ch from hook (counts as 1hdc), 1hdc into next ch, [1dc into each of next 2 ch, 1hdc into each of next 2 ch, 1sc into each of next 2 ch, 1hdc into each of next 2 ch] 5 times, turn. (42 sts)

Row 2: ch1, work into blo, except for the first and last dc of the row, 1dc into each of next 2 sts, [1tr into each of next 2 sts, 1dc into each of next 2 sts, 1sc into each of next 2 sts, 1dc into each of next 2 sts] 5 times, turn. (42 sts)

Row 3: ch1, work through both loops of each st, 1dc into each of next 2 sts [1tr into each of next 2 sts, 1dc into each of next 2 sts, 1sc into each of next 2 sts, 1dc into each of next 2 sts] 5 times, turn. (42 sts)

Rows 4–23: repeat Rows 2–3 10 more times.

Row 24: repeat Row 2.

Row 25: ch1, work through both loops of each st, 1hdc into each of next 2 sts, [1dc into each of next 2 sts, 1hdc into each of next 2 sts, 1sc into each of next 2 sts, 1hdc into each of next 2 sts] 5 times, turn.

To make the edging

Change to size M/N-13 (9 mm) hook.

Round 1: ch1, *[1sc, ch1, 1sc] into next st, pm into last ch-1 sp (corner), ch1, 1sc into next st, ch1, [skip 1 st, 1sc into next st, ch1] rep until 2 sts remain along edge, 1sc into next st, ch1, [1sc, ch1, 1sc] into base of last st, pm into last ch-1 sp (corner); rotate to work along the side edge, ch1 skip 1 row, [1sc into edge of next row, ch1] 23 times, skip 1 row**; rotate to work along remaining loops of the foundation chain sts, rep from * to ** once more; sl st into first sc to join.

Remove stitch marker before working into marked sp and place as indicated.

Round 2: sl st into marked corner-sp, ch1, [1sc,

ch1, 1sc] into same corner-sp, pm into last ch-1 sp (corner), *ch1, [1sc into next ch-1 sp, ch 1] rep to next stitch marker, [1sc, ch1, 1sc] into corner-sp, pm into last ch-1 sp (corner) *; rep from * to * twice more, [1sc into next ch-1 sp, ch1] to end of round, sl st into first sc to join.

Rounds 3–4: repeat Round 2 twice.
Fasten off.

FINISHING
Weave in loose ends.

If making your own pillow cover
To make the square on which to stitch the crochet panel, take the piece of sturdy upholstery fabric. The fabric should measure the size of the crochet pillow panel plus 1" (2.5 cm) seam allowance along each edge for the front, plus 2.5 times the size of the cushion cover to make the back overlapping section.

Hem the two shortest edges by folding the edge over by 1" (2.5 cm) twice and then, topstitching along the bottom edge of the seam. This will give you a neat seam that does not require serging.

Fold the fabric in half lengthwise and locate the center. Use dressmaker's pins to mark 11" (28 cm) in on either side of this fold, along the top and the bottom edges of the fabric. Unfold the fabric. You should now have a 22" (56 cm) square pinned in the middle of the fabric. With right sides facing, and using the pins as guides, fold one seamed edge three-quarters of the way onto the center square. Fold the other seamed edge three-quarters of the way over the center square as well so that the two folded parts overlap each other.

With right sides facing, pin all three layers together along the top and the bottom of the folded square, 1" (2.5 cm) in from the edge of the fabric. Sew along these lines to create the pillow cover. Trim away excess edging to leave a ¼" (6 mm) seam allowance.

Turn the pillow cover right-side out. Position the crochet panel onto the front of the cushion cover and pin in place. Using whip stitch, hand stitch the back of the crochet stitches to the pillow cover.

Feel-good tip

The tactile shell stitch used in this pattern echoes the rippling waves and colors of the sand. Take your pillow with you when you want to meditate outside in comfort and feel refreshed by the natural world around you.

Tip
If you don't like
sewing, make two
crochet panels and join
them together using
slip stitch.

Explore

Designed to be used while traveling, this exercise will help you find calm and reduce anxiety as you travel, whether you are journeying near or far. You can use any small, portable crochet pattern for this exercise, like the ones on pages 58–63.

1 Take out a portable crochet project and begin stitching. Use the position of your hands to mark your personal boundary. Create a space within which you feel safe and still.

2 Retain a light awareness of your environment around this space. It is a quiet, contemplative, focused place that is yours and yours alone.

3 Focus on the yarn running through your fingers, and as the yarn unwinds, so does your mind. Fix your gaze on the movements of your hands. The hustle, bustle, and noise around you retreat into the background.

4 Notice your thoughts come and go. If thoughts of the journey or the people around you encroach on your quietness, gently bring them back to the rhythm of your hands and the safety of your space.

5 Notice the rhythm of your breath. Do not force it, simply let it do its job. As you relax into your space, allow your breathing to become quiet.

6 Notice any tension in your shoulders and jaw and relax your muscles.

7 If anxious thoughts emerge, simply observe them. They are merely thoughts conjured up by your mind. Nothing more. Let them go.

8 Enjoy the experience of your body and mind working together in complete harmony and safety.

9 As you near the end of your journey, spend a few minutes remembering this feeling of security and calm. Let it be your sanctuary in the future.

Sleep Tight Eye Mask Set

Creating this eye mask and pouch set is a wonderful opportunity to find peace and calm in the busyness of everyday life while making a practical item to help you relax on future trips.

YOU WILL NEED

* DK-weight, wool/acrylic/ cashmere blend yarn (approx. 1¾ oz/50 g; 137 yds/125 m) MC 1 ball in blue
* Scraps of DK-weight, wool/ acrylic/cashmere blend yarns CCa dark pink CCb pink CCc burgundy
* Cotton lining fabric, 9½ x 8½" (24 x 21.5 cm)
* Size D-3 (3.25 mm) hook
* Yarn needle
* Suede cord, 26" (66 cm)
* Zipper, 10" (25 cm)
* Sewing needle and matching sewing thread
* Dressmaker's pins

GAUGE

* Eye Mask: 26 sc and 29 rows measure 4" (10 cm).
* Pouch: three mandalas measure 4½" (11.5 cm); strip of mandalas measures 1¼" (3 cm) wide.

DIMENSIONS

* Eye mask: 3¾" (9.5 cm) wide, 8" (20 cm) long.
* Pouch: 9" (23 cm) wide, 4" (10 cm) deep.

TO MAKE THE EYE MASK

Using MC, ch13.

Row 1: 1sc into second ch from hook (counts as 1sc), 1sc into each ch to end, turn. (12 sts)

Row 2: ch1, 2sc into next st, 1sc into each of next 10 sts, 2sc into next st, turn. (14 sts)

Row 3: ch1, 2sc into next st, 1sc into each of next 12 sts, 2sc into next st, turn. (16 sts)

Row 4: ch1, 2sc into next st, 1sc into each of next 14 sts, 2sc into next st, turn. (18 sts)

Row 5: ch1, 2sc into next st, 1sc into each of next 16 sts, 2sc into next st, turn. (20 sts)

Row 6: ch1, 2sc into next st, 1sc into each of next 18 sts, 2sc into next st, turn. (22 sts)

Rows 7–21: ch1, 1sc into each st, turn. (22 sts)

Row 22: ch1, sc2tog, 1sc into each of next 18 sts, sc2tog, turn. (20 sts)

Row 23: ch1, sc2tog, 1sc into each of next 16 sts, sc2tog, turn. (18 sts)

Row 24: ch1, sc2tog, 1sc into each of next 14 sts, sc2tog, turn. (16 sts)

Row 25: ch1, sc2tog, 1sc into each of next 12 sts, sc2tog, turn. (14 sts)

Row 26: ch1, 1sc into each st, turn. (14 sts)

Rows 27–49: repeat Rows 3–25.

Row 50: ch1, sc2tog, 1sc into each of next 10 sts, sc2tog. (12 sts)

Fasten off.

To make the edging

Using CCa, join yarn to first st of one short end.

Round 1: ch1, 2sc into first st, 1sc into each of next 10 sts, 2sc into last st; rotate to work along the top edge, 2sc into first row, 1sc into each of next 48 rows, 2sc into last row; rotate to work along the short end, 2sc into first st, 1sc into each of next 10 sts, 2sc into last st; rotate to work along bottom edge, 2sc into first row, 1sc into each of next 48 rows, 2sc into last row. Fasten off.

To make the scalloped edgings

Using CCa, join yarn to the first st of edging along one short end.

Row 1: 5dc into first sc, [sl st into next sc, skip 1 st, 5dc into next sc] 4 times, sl st into last sc. Fasten off. Weave in loose ends.

Repeat for the second short end.

FINISHING

The cord will now be attached to the right-hand side of the mask at the top and bottom corners. Weave the other end of the cord through the left-hand side of the mask in the same way. Take the end of the cord on the left-hand side of the mask and tie in an adjustable knot around the cord near the top corner on the right-hand side of the mask (see the photograph on page 56 for reference). Then take the end of the cord on the right-hand side of the mask and tie in an adjustable knot around the cord near the top corner on the left-hand side.

TO MAKE THE EYE MASK POUCH
To make the center strip (make 2)
Using CCa, make a magic ring.

Round 1: ch2 (do not count), 10dc into ring, sl st into top of first dc to join.

Round 2: ch2 (do not count), 2dc into each st to end of round, sl st into top of first dc to join. (20 sts)

Fasten off.

**To make the next mandala:
Using CCa, make a magic ring.

Round 1: ch2 (do not count), 10dc into ring, sl st to first dc to join.

Round 2: ch2 (do not count), sl st into top loops of tenth st of last round of last mandala made, [2dc into next st] 10 times, sl st into top of first dc to join. (20 sts)

Fasten off.

Repeat from ** 4 times more. (6 circles)

To make the edging
Join MC to outer edge of mandala on right hand edge of strip into dc opposite join.

Round 1: *ch3, [1tr into next st, 1dc into next st, 1hdc into next st, 1sc into each of next 4 sts, 1hdc into next st, 1dc into next st, 1tr into next st] 6 times, ch3, sl st into next st of last mandala*, rotate to work along bottom edge, rep from * to * once more.

Fasten off.

To make the top strip (make 2)
Using CCb, work mandala strip as for center strip.
Using MC, work edging as for center strip.

To make the lower strip (make 2)
Using CCc, work mandala strip as for center strip.
Using MC, work edging as for center strip.

FINISHING
To assemble the front panel
Join one each of the top, center, and lower strips together to form the front panel. First, hold one of the top strips and one of the center strips with the wrong sides together. Join MC to the right-hand corner of one long edge and then slip stitch along the length of the edge making sure to work into both strips.

Fasten off.

Hold the joined strip with one of the lower strips with wrong sides together. Attach the lower strip to the other side of the center strip in the same way.

To assemble the back panel
Repeat the joining process for the front panel.

To join the front and back panels
Hold the front and back panels together with wrong sides facing each other.
Join MC into first st of left-hand short end.
Row 1: working into both the next st on the panel in front and the corresponding st on the panel behind, *2sc into first st, 1sc into each st to last st, 2sc into next st*; rotate to work along bottom edge, rep from * to *; rotate to work along right-hand edge, rep from * to *, rotate to work along top edge, working through front panel only, rep from * to * once more, sl st into first sc to join.
Fasten off.

Join MC into first st of remaining top edge.
Repeat from * to * once more.
Fasten off. Weave in loose ends.

To make the lining
Place the zipper face up onto the right side of the cotton fabric, along one of the 9½" (24 cm) edges—aligning the outer edge of the zipper tape with the outer edge of the fabric and the top of the zipper with one 8½" (21.5 cm) edge. Pin and sew the zipper edge in place. Fold the cotton fabric in half, right side together. With the right side of the remaining 9½" (24 cm) edge and the wrong side of the zipper together, pin and sew the remaining zipper edge in place. Trim the zipper length. Flatten the fabric tube so that the zipper is along one edge.

Using a ¼" (6 mm) seam allowance, pin, and sew the two open ends closed.

Place the lining inside the crochet pouch, pin, and sew along the zipper tapes to the top edge of the pouch.

Feel-good tip

As you create your eye mask, the rhythmic movement of your hands will help you to experience calm on your journey. When it is complete, your eye mask will enable you to rest peacefully on your travels.

Safe Document Wallet

There is an ease to crocheting this wallet pattern that makes it a great portable way to find calm on the go, whether you are traveling, commuting, or just waiting for friends. The colors are designed to keep you engaged, and crocheting the simple rhythmic pattern will help you center your thoughts while out and about.

YOU WILL NEED

* Worsted-weight wool yarn (approx. 1¾ oz/50 g; 65 yds/60 m)
CCa 2 balls in gold
CCb 1 ball in jade
CCc 1 ball in amethyst
CCd 1 ball in navy

* Size N/P-15 (10 mm) hook

* Yarn needle

* Stiff iron-on interfacing, 2 pieces 10 × 13½" (25 × 34.25 cm)

* Cotton lining fabric, 2 pieces 10½ × 14". (26.5 × 35.5 cm)

* Clothes iron

* Sewing needle and matching sewing thread

* Dressmaker's pins

GAUGE

12 sts and 11 rows measure 4" (10 cm) over pattern.

DIMENSIONS

10" (25.5 cm) wide, 13½" (34 cm) deep.

TO MAKE THE FRONT PANEL

Using CCa, ch29.

Row 1: 1sc into second ch from hook (counts as 1sc), 1dc into next ch, [1sc into next ch, 1dc into foll ch] rep to end, turn. (28 sts)

Row 2: ch1, [1sc into next st, 1dc into foll st] rep to end, turn.

The last 2 rows set the stitch pattern. Each row should start with 1sc and end with 1dc.

Rows 3–4: repeat Row 2 twice more.

Join in CCb.

Rows 5–8: using CCb, repeat Row 2 4 more times.

Rows 9–12: using CCa, repeat Row 2 4 more times.

Join in CCc.

Rows 13–16: using CCc, repeat Row 2 4 more times.

Rows 17–20: using CCa, repeat Row 2 4 more times.

Join in CCd.

Rows 21–24: using CCd, repeat Row 2 4 more times.

Rows 25–28: using CCa, repeat Row 2 4 more times.

Rows 29–32: using CCb, repeat Row 2 4 more times.

Rows 33–36: using CCa, repeat Row 2 4 more times.

Fasten off.

TO MAKE THE BACK PANEL

Work as front.

FINISHING

To join the front and back panels

Hold the front and back panels together with wrong sides facing each other.

Join CCc through both panels at the right-hand corner at beginning of bottom edge.

Row 1: working through both panels, 2sc into first st, 1sc into each of next 26 sts, 2sc into last st of bottom edge (30 sts); rotate to work along side edge, 1sc into each row along the edge (36 sts); rotate to work along top edge, working through front panel only (top edge), 2sc into first st, 1sc into each of the next 26 sts,

2sc into last st of front edge; rotate to work along remaining edge, working through both layers of fabric, 1sc into each row along the edge (36 sts).
Fasten off.
Join CCc to right-hand corner of remaining top edge.
Top Back: working through one layer of fabric, 2sc into first st, 1sc into each of next 26 sts, 2sc into last st of back edge.
Fasten off. Weave in loose ends.

To reinforce the document wallet
Following the interfacing instructions, attach one piece of interfacing to the middle of the wrong side of each piece of cotton fabric. Fold ¼" (6 mm) of cotton fabric along one 10½" (26.5 cm) edge to the wrong side on each piece of cotton fabric, pin and sew in place. Place both pieces right sides together, with the hemmed edges together and pin in place. Using a ¼" (6 mm) seam allowance, sew along the remaining three unworked edges. Place inside the Document Wallet and hand stitch to the top edge at the opening of the wallet.

Tip
To hold your documents in place, attach a button loop and button to the top edge of your wallet.

Feel-good tip

Practice recalling the feelings of tranquility evoked in the exercise so that even when you don't have your crochet immediately on hand you can still experience the same sense of calm. Your projects will serve as a physical reminder of this peaceful, safe space.

Refresh

Taking a short break from your working day does wonders to improve your well-being and ability to work. Return refreshed and ready to face the world.

1 Find a place away from your work environment, if only for 10–15 minutes.

2 Sit quietly with your crochet. Take a moment to focus on your hands and their rhythmic calming movements. Welcome the familiar sense of comfort it brings.

3 When you feel settled, focus on your body. Take note of any tension in the muscles and let it go, especially in your shoulder girdle, neck, and jaw line. Gently relax your mouth. Feel the furrow leave your brow.

4 Ease your grip on your hook and be aware of your own tension being reflected in your stitches. As one relaxes so will the other.

5 Feel the rhythm of your hands sync with your internal rhythm, and as you do so, experience the stress of the day leave your mind and body.

6 Observe your breathing rate slowing down and your heart rate gently easing, becoming steady and relaxed. Notice how different this feels.

7 Feel the tactile sensation of the yarn and the three-dimensional nature of the movement. It feels very different from your work-related activities. It's a welcome mini break for your mind.

8 Engage with any creative thoughts and allow them to blossom. Solutions to problems you've been mulling over may well spring to mind as you take focus away from work.

9 When your available time is up, gently stretch your hands and shoulders and take a short stroll to stimulate your circulation before returning to work feeling refreshed.

No Stress Balls

Creating these stress balls will gently lull your mind into a peaceful rhythm as your stitches spiral around. Keep a stress ball on your desk as a reminder to take a moment to yourself each day.

YOU WILL NEED

* Scraps of DK-weight, wool/acrylic/cashmere blend yarns in assorted colors
* Size E-4 (3.5 mm) hook
* Fiberfill
* Stitch marker
* Yarn needle

GAUGE

20 sc and 22 rows measure 4" (10 cm).

DIMENSIONS*

* Extra Small Ball 1" (2.5 cm) in diameter.
* Small Ball 1¾" (4.5 cm) in diameter.
* Medium Ball 2¾" (7 cm) in diameter.
* Large Ball 3½" (9 cm) in diameter.

* Only approximate measurements can be given because the size of the finished project will vary depending on the gauge and the amount of fiberfill used.

NOTES

* Stuff the balls as lightly or as tightly as you wish.
* When making the balls you will be working in spiral rounds. Do not work a sl st at the end of each round to join the round to the first st.
* Place a stitch marker in last st of each round. Remove the st marker before working the st and replace st marker after completing the new st.

TO MAKE AN EXTRA SMALL BALL

Using color of choice, make a magic ring.

Round 1 (RS): 6sc into ring.

Round 2: 2sc into each st to end of round. (12 sts)

Rounds 3–5: 1sc into each st to end of round. Stuff ball with fiberfill.

Round 6: [sc2tog flo over next 2 sts] 6 times. (6 sts)

Fasten off.

Weave loose end through each stitch around the opening and draw the stitches together. Weave in loose ends and squeeze ball to shape.

TO MAKE A SMALL BALL

Using color of choice, make a magic ring.

Round 1 (RS): 8sc into ring.

Round 2: [1sc into next st, 2sc into next st] 4 times. (12 sts)

Round 3: [1sc into next st, 2sc into next st] 6 times. (18 sts)

Round 4: [1sc into each of next 2 sts, 2sc into next st] 6 times. (24 sts)

Rounds 5–8: 1sc into each st to end of round.

Round 9: [1sc into each of next 2 sts, sc2tog flo over next 2 sts] 6 times. (18 sts)

Round 10: [1sc into next st, sc2tog flo over next 2 sts] 6 times. (12 sts)

Stuff ball with fiberfill.

Round 11: [sc2tog flo over next 2 sts] 6 times. (6 sts)

Stuff ball with more fiberfill if needed.

Fasten off.

Weave loose end through each stitch around the opening and draw the stitches together. Weave in loose ends and squeeze ball to shape.

TO MAKE A MEDIUM BALL

Using color of choice, make a magic ring.

Round 1 (RS): 8sc into ring.

Round 2: [1sc into next st, 2sc into next st] 4 times. (12 sts)

Round 3: [1sc into next st, 2sc into next st] 6 times. (18 sts)

Round 4: [1sc into each of next 2 sts, 2sc into next st] 6 times. (24 sts)

Round 5: [1sc into each of next 2 sts, 2sc into next st] 8 times. (32 sts)

Round 6: [1sc into each of next 3 sts, 2sc into next st] 8 times. (40 sts)

Rounds 7–12: 1sc into each st to end of round.

Round 13: [1sc into each of next 3 sts, sc2tog flo over next 2 sts] 8 times. (32 sts)

Round 14: [1sc into each of next 2 sts, sc2tog flo over next 2 sts] 8 times. (24 sts)

Round 15: [1sc into each of next 2 sts, sc2tog flo over next 2 sts] 6 times. (18 sts)

Stuff ball with fiberfill.

Round 16: [1sc into next st, sc2tog flo over next 2 sts] 6 times. (12 sts)

Stuff ball with more fiberfill if needed.

Round 17: [sc2tog flo over next 2 sts] 6 times. (6 sts)

Fasten off.

Weave loose end through each stitch around the opening and draw the stitches together. Weave in loose ends and squeeze ball to shape.

TO MAKE A LARGE BALL

Using color of choice, make a magic ring.

Round 1 (RS): 8sc into ring.

Round 2: [1sc into next st, 2sc into next st] 4 times. (12 sts)

Round 3: [1sc into next st, 2sc into next st] 6 times. (18 sts)

Round 4: [1sc into each of next 2 sts, 2sc into next st] 6 times. (24 sts)

Round 5: [1sc into each of next 2 sts, 2sc into next st] 8 times. (32 sts)

Round 6: [1sc into each of next 3 sts, 2sc into next st] 8 times. (40 sts)

Round 7: [1sc into each of next 3 sts, 2sc into next st] 10 times. (50 sts)

Rounds 8–17: 1sc into each st to end of round.

Round 18: [1sc into each of next 3 sts, sc2tog flo over next 2 sts] 10 times. (40 sts)

Round 19: [1sc into each of next 3 sts, sc2tog flo over next 2 sts] 8 times. (32 sts)

Round 20: [1sc into each of next 2 sts, sc2tog flo over next 2 sts] 8 times. (24 sts)

Stuff ball with fiberfill.

Round 21: [1sc into each of next 2 sts, sc2tog flo over next 2 sts] 6 times. (18 sts)

Stuff ball with more fiberfill if needed.

Round 22: [1sc into next st, sc2tog flo over next 2 sts] 6 times. (12 sts)

Round 23: [sc2tog over next 2 sts] 6 times. (6 sts)

Fasten off.

Weave loose end through each stitch around the opening and draw the stitches together. Weave in loose ends and squeeze ball to shape.

Feel-good tip

Use your stress balls wherever work takes you. Keep a set on your desk and in your bag. When you need a helping hand to manage stress or anger, give them a squeeze and recall the calm you felt while making them.

Colorful Coasters

Based on mandalas that represent unity, harmony, and wholeness, these colorful coasters will enable you to find balance, too.

YOU WILL NEED

* DK-weight, wool/acrylic/ cashmere blend yarns (approx. 1¾ oz/50 g; 137 yds/125 m)
CCa 1 ball in orange
CCb 1 ball in bright pink
CCc 1 ball in teal
CCd 1 ball in pink
CCe 1 ball in yellow
CCf 1 ball in pale blue
CCg 1 ball in pale green
CCh 1 ball in white
CCi 1 ball in pale pink
CCj 1 ball in coral

* Size E-4 (3.5 mm) hook
* Yarn needle
* Safety pins

GAUGE

Gauge is not important in the project.

DIMENSIONS

* 4½" (11.5 cm) in diameter.

TO MAKE A PALE PINK FLOWER COASTER

Base

Using CCf, make a magic ring.

Round 1 (RS): ch3 (counts as first dc), 11dc into the ring, sl st into top of beg ch-3 to join. (12 sts)

Round 2: ch3 (counts as first dc), 1dc into base of beg ch-3, 2dc into each st to end of round, sl st into top of beg ch-3 to join. (24 sts)

Round 3: ch3 (counts as first dc), 1dc into base of beg ch-3, 1dc into next st, [2dc into next st, 1dc into next st] 11 times, sl st into top of beg ch-3 to join. (36 sts)

Round 4: ch3 (counts as first dc), 1dc into base of beg ch-3, 1dc into each of next 2 sts, [2dc into next st, 1dc into each of the next 2 sts] 11 times, sl st into top of beg ch-3 to join. (48 sts)

Round 5: ch3 (counts as first dc), 1dc into base of beg ch-3, 1dc into each of next 3 sts, [2dc into next st, 1dc into each of the next 3 sts] 11 times, sl st into top of beg ch-3 to join. (60 sts)
Fasten off. Weave in loose ends.

Top

Using CCe, make a magic ring.

Round 1 (RS): ch3 (counts as first dc), 11dc into the ring, sl st into top of beg ch-3 to join. (12 sts)

Round 2: ch3 (counts as first dc), 1dc into base of beg ch-3, 2dc into each st to end of round, sl st into top of beg ch-3 to join. (24 sts)
Fasten off CCe. Join CCi to the top of any dc st.

Round 3: ch1 (counts as first sc), 1hdc into base of beg ch-1, *work [1dc, 1tr, 1dc] into next st, into next st work [1hdc, 1sc], work [1sc, 1hdc] into next st; rep from * 6 times more, work [1dc, 1tr, 1dc] into next st, work [1hdc, 1sc] into next st, sl st into top of beg ch-1 to join. (8 petals)
Fasten off CCi. Join CCg to the top of any tr st.

Round 4: [ch6, skip 6 sts, sl st to top of next tr] 7 times, ch6, sl st into base of beg ch-6 to join. (8 ch-sp)

Round 5: sl st into ch-6 sp, ch2 (counts as first hdc), 8hdc into same sp, [1hdc into next sl st, 9hdc into next ch-6 sp] 7 times, sl st into top of beg ch-2 to join. (80 sts)
Fasten off.

Finishing

Weave in loose ends.

With wrong sides together place the Top onto the Base, ensuring that the middles meet and pin into place.

Join in CCj, through both the Top and the Base, in a stitch space between two stitches on Round 5. Using the photograph opposite as a guide, working into the stitch spaces between the stitches on Round 5, slip stitch (or alternatively sew, using a back stitch) the Top and Base together so that the Top sits just inside the edge of the Base.

TO MAKE AN ORANGE FLOWER COASTER

Work as for the pale pink flower coaster, replacing the yarns with the yarns indicated.

Base

Work as for the pale pink flower coaster, using CCd.

Top

Using CCe, make a magic ring.

Rounds 1–2: using CCe.

Round 3: using CCa.

Rounds 4–5: using CCh.

Finishing

Join the top and the base using CCb.

TO MAKE A BLUE FLOWER COASTER

Work as for the pale pink flower coaster, replacing the yarns with the yarns indicated.

Base

Work as for the pale pink flower coaster, using CCg.

Top

Using CCe, make a magic ring.

Rounds 1–2: using CCe.

Round 3: using CCf.

Rounds 4–5: using CCa.

Finishing

Join the top and the base using CCc.

TO MAKE A DARK PINK FLOWER COASTER

Work as for the pale pink flower coaster, replacing the yarns with the yarns indicated.

Base

Work as for the pale pink flower coaster, using CCj.

Top

Using CCe, make a magic ring.

Rounds 1–2: using CCe.

Round 3: using CCb.

Rounds 4–5: using CCc.

Finishing

Join the top and the base using CCh.

Feel-good tip

Keep your stress-relieving project on your desk at work to manage the tensions of the day. The bright cheerful colors and pattern will serve as a reminder to manage your stress on a daily basis.

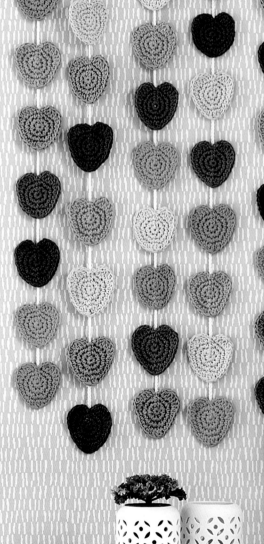

Dream

Choose a quiet, safe space to practice this exercise as you crochet. Allow yourself plenty of time for your dreams to develop and inspire.

1 As your hands begin their rhythmic work, notice your breath and feel the calmness of this moment infuse your soul. Give yourself permission to daydream.

2 Focus on the steady, strong rhythm of your heart and begin to nurture those hidden dreams held within—your heart's desires.

3 Softly begin to explore the aspirations you've held there, and as you do so, feel your thoughts gently untether from the demands and problems of the world.

4 Allow your dreams to grow and flow. Feel them expand beyond the confines of your body into the space around you. There are no restrictions.

5 Take time to enjoy the sensation of thoughts that are completely free from the constraints of your daily routines.

6 Notice an emerging sense of excitement as your imagination opens up new doors, fresh possibilities, and pathways. Allow yourself the confidence to explore these further.

7 As your confidence grows, you will begin to feel strong and able. Be aware of a renewed sense of who you truly are. Discover your inner strength.

8 You are a wonderfully unique human being. Focus on your skill and the beautiful work you are able to create. Realize your full potential, because you can. Acknowledge what's in your heart.

9 Drift back to the real world with a desire to live life fully, to make the most of every precious moment. Make the decision to explore and enjoy the wonderful opportunities life has to offer.

Follow Your Heart Wall Hanging

This simple heart motif is worked in the round with the classic heart shape added to the outer round using a mix of increasing and decreasing techniques. Additional hearts and strings can be added to change the size of the wall hanging (see the full hanging on page 72).

YOU WILL NEED

* Scraps of DK-weight, cotton yarn
For heart motifs in:
CC pink
CC yellow
CC pale blue
CC dark blue green
CC gray
CC purple
CC turquoise
For hanging string in:
MC ecru

* Size G-6 (4 mm) hook
* Yarn needle
* Dressmaker's pins
* Sewing needle and thread

GAUGE

Gauge is not important in the project, but be aware the string will stretch a little once the hearts are added.

DIMENSIONS

* Heart: 2½" (6.5 cm) square.
* Wall hanging: 18" (46 cm) wide, 27" (69 cm) long.

TO MAKE A HEART MOTIF (MAKE 40 IN A RANGE OF COLORS)

Using color of choice, make a magic ring.

Round 1: ch1, 8sc into ring, sl st into beg ch-1 to join. (8 sts)

Round 2: ch1, 2sc into each st to end of round, sl st into beg ch-1 to join. (16 sts)

Round 3: ch1, [1sc into next st, 2sc into next st] 8 times, sl st into beg ch-1 to join. (24 sts)

Round 4: ch3 (counts as first dc), dc3tog over next 3 sts, 2dc into next st, 2hdc into next st, 1sc into each of next 5 sts, work [dc2tog over next 2 sts] twice, 1sc into each of next 5 sts, 2hdc into next st, 2dc into next st, dc3tog over last 3 sts, ch3, sl st into same place as sl st from previous round.

Fasten off. Weave in loose ends.

TO MAKE THE TOP SECTION

Using MC, ch101.

Row 1: 1sc into second ch from hook (counts as 1sc), 1sc into each ch to end, turn. (100 sts)

Row 2: ch1, 1sc into each st to end, turn.

Rows 3–4: repeat Row 2 twice more.

To make the top section longer work more rows at this point.

Fasten off.

TO MAKE A HANGING STRING (MAKE 5)

Using MC, ch140 or work a chain approximately 25" (63.5 cm) long.

Fasten off.

FINISHING

Block and press each heart to approximately 2½" (6.5 cm). Block and press top section and each hanging string to the same length. Weave in loose ends.

Lay out the hearts in five groups of eight and experiment with the placement of colors to ensure that the colors are evenly distributed. Starting with the bottom heart, place the hearts onto the hanging strings, making sure they are as evenly spaced as possible, and leaving approximately 2" (5 cm) at the top of each hanging string to attach it to the top section.

Once you are happy with the placement, pin the hearts in position and sew them in place. Starting with the center hanging string, pin and

stitch to the center point of the top section. Place the outer hanging strings approximately 20 stitches in from the ends and evenly space the remaining hanging strings in-between. Pin and stitch in place.

To make the hanging loops

Fold the outer edges of the top section over by approximately 2" (5cm). Pin and stitch in place.

Feel-good tip

The day-to-day routine of life can become a habit that quashes our dreams. Hang your hearts somewhere where you will see them often. They will remind you to take note of what's in your heart, be true to it, and live life to your full potential. Be inspired!

Blue Sky Afghan

This project involves a range of techniques. The background is created using half double crochet throughout and can be made to any size. Worked individually, the clouds are appliquéd in place. Carry materials for the clouds in your bag to create when you are out and about.

YOU WILL NEED
* DK-weight, wool blend yarn 100% wool, (approx. 1¾ oz/50 g; 122½ yds/112 m)
* For a baby afghan size:
MC 10 balls in blue
CC 1 ball in white
* For a crib afghan size:
MC 16 balls in blue
CC 2 balls in white
* For a lap afghan size:
MC 23 balls in blue
CC 3 balls in white
* Size G-6 (4 mm) hook
* Yarn needle
* Dressmaker's pins
* Sewing needle and thread

GAUGE
Before blocking: 16 hdc and 10 rows measure 4" (10 cm).
After blocking: 14 hdc and 9 rows measure 4" (10 cm).

DIMENSIONS
* Baby: 36" (90 cm) square.
* Crib: 45" (112.5 cm) square.
* Lap: 54" (135 cm) square.

NOTES
* If the chain or stitch count differs for each size, the counts are given together, in order of project size as follows: Baby (Crib, Lap).
* The number of Clouds you will need depends on the size of afghan. Start by making 24 Clouds, place them onto the afghan and make more as required.

TO MAKE THE AFGHAN
Using MC, ch128 (160, 191).
Row 1: 1hdc into third ch from hook (counts as 1hdc), 1hdc into each ch to end, turn. (126 (158, 189 sts))
Row 2: ch2, 1hdc into base of beg ch-2, 1hdc into each st to end, turn.
Repeat Row 2 until afghan is required length. Fasten off.

TO MAKE A CLOUD MOTIF
Using CC, ch10.
Row 1: 1sc into second ch from hook, 1sc into each ch to end, turn. (9 sts)
Row 2: ch1, 2sc into next st, 1sc into each st, until 1 st remains, 2sc into last st, turn. (11 sts)

Row 3: skip 1 st, 5hdc into next st, 1sc into each of next 5 sts, skip 1 st, work [1hdc, 6dc] into next st, skip 1 st, sl st into last st, turn.
Row 4: sl st into each of next 6 sts, skip 2 sts, 7dc into next st, skip 2 sts, sl st into next st. Fasten off.

FINISHING
Block and press the afghan to the required size, being careful not to overstretch the fabric. Block and press the clouds into shape. Weave in all loose ends.
Place the clouds onto the afghan, starting the first row approximately 4" (10 cm) from the bottom edge and approximately 2" (5 cm) from the sides. Once you are happy with the positioning, pin and stitch them into place.

Feel-good tip

Let this project be your key to a new way of thinking; like the sky, free of limitations, open minded, creative, liberating. Explore this new blue-sky thinking and allow it to help you to achieve your dreams.

Focus

Discover focus and flow in the everlasting projects on the following pages. Let the process of creation be your constant friend in the background of your life.

1 Take your thoughts to the color of your yarn. Examine how you feel and choose a tone that reflects your mood at this moment.

2 Notice the yarn's texture. Reflect on how it makes you feel as you touch it.

3 As you begin your crochet, notice the difference between the softness of the yarn and the strength of your hook. Observe your hook moving in and out as the yarn winds around and off. The world retreats as you focus on the process at hand.

4 Feel your hands move effortlessly and automatically in a rhythmic flow of movement that emerges from your subconscious. They weave their magic without the need for conscious interference.

5 Loosely notice the structure of each stitch but if you see an error do not be tempted to undo it. Let it go in the knowledge that it makes your project beautifully unique, just like you. Celebrate its uniqueness—it will tell your story.

6 Experience total absorption in the process. Feel your mind flow into its everlasting rhythm, and as you do so experience time itself appear to stop in this moment of complete focus.

7 Your focus is such that it enables you to feel energized, positive, joyful, and stress free.

8 Feel totally at one with the process of creating and utterly absorbed in the moment.

9 Stay in this space for as long as you need.

Everlasting Lap Afghan

Add to your afghan whenever you feel the urge. This project will grow with you, telling your story in its never-ending rows of stitches. Have fun choosing colors to reflect your current mood.

YOU WILL NEED

* Worsted-weight, acrylic/wool blend yarn (approx. 3 oz/85 g; 197 yds/180 m)
CCa 3 balls in cream
CCb 2 balls in light blue
CCc 2 balls in navy
CCd 1 ball in mid-blue*
* Size H-8 (5 mm) hook
* Yarn needle

GAUGE

1 chevron repeat (32 sts) and 9 rows measure 6½" (16.5 cm) over pattern.

DIMENSIONS

41" (104 cm) wide, 42" (107 cm) long.*

*The yarn quantities given here are to make the afghan at the specified size. As this is an everlasting project, it is up to you how large or small your afghan is and this will determine how much yarn is required.

SPECIAL STITCHES

3dc-dec: [yrh, insert hook into next st, yrh, pull up through st, yrh, pull through two loops] 3 times, yrh, pull through all loops. Do not finish with chain stitch.

5dc-dec: [yrh, insert hook into next st, yrh, pull up through st, yrh, pull through two loops] 5 times, yrh, pull through all loops. Do not finish with chain stitch.

NOTE

The ch-3 at the beginning of each row does not count as a stitch and should not be worked.

TO MAKE THE LAP AFGHAN

Using CCa, ch191.

Row 1: 1dc into fourth ch from hook, 1dc into each of next 12 ch, 5dc into next ch, [1dc into each of next 13 ch, 5dc-dec over next 5 ch, 1dc into each of next 13 ch, 5dc into next ch] 5 times, 1dc into each of next 14 sts, turn.

Row 2: ch3 (do not count as st), 3dc-dec over next 3 sts, 1dc into each of next 13 sts, 5dc into next st, [1dc into each of next 13 sts, 5dc-dec over next 5 sts, 1dc into each of next 13 sts, 5dc into next st] 5 times, 1dc into each of next 13 sts, 3dc-dec over next 3 sts.

Rows 3–6: repeat Row 2.
****Fasten off CCa. Join in CCb.

Rows 7–12: repeat Row 2.
Fasten off CCb. Join in CCc.

Rows 13–18: repeat Row 2. ******
Fasten off CCc. Join in CCa.

Rows 19–24: repeat Row 2.
Fasten off CCa. Join in CCd.

Rows 25–30: repeat Row 2.
Fasten off CCd. Join in CCa.

Rows 31–36: repeat Row 2.
Repeat from ** until the work measures approximately 42" (107 cm) from the foundation chain or the desired length is reached. This is an everlasting project so it can be as large or as small as you like—simply keep adding rows until you feel that the project has come to a natural finish.
Fasten off. Weave in loose ends.

Tip

Work the final stage of the decreases by easing the hook through a few loops at a time.

Hexagonal Rug

Created from hexagons in super bulky yarn, this makes a thick sturdy rug
that you can add to whenever you please.

YOU WILL NEED

* Super bulky-weight, acrylic/wool blend yarn (approx. 6 oz/170 g; 106 yds/97 m)
CCa 3 balls in purple
CCb 2 balls in lime green
Ccc 2 balls in dark purple*
* Size M/N-13 (9 mm) hook
* Yarn needle

GAUGE

One hexagon measures 9½" (24 cm) from point to point using two strands of yarn.

DIMENSIONS

24" (61 cm) wide, 43" (109 cm) long.*

* Each ball of yarn will make two hexagons. The yarn quantities given here are to make the rug at the specified size. As this is an everlasting project, it is up to you how large or small your rug is and this will determine how much yarn is required.

NOTE

Each ball of yarn makes two hexagons.

TO MAKE THE HEXAGON RUG

Using the color of choice and two strands of yarn held together, ch4 (counts as 1dc and 1ch).

Round 1: [1dc, ch1] 5 times into fourth ch from hook, sl st into third ch of beg ch-4 to join.

Round 2: ch3 (counts as first dc), *[1dc, ch1, 1dc] into ch-1 sp, 1dc into next st; rep from * 4 times more, [1dc, ch1, 1dc] into ch-1 sp, sl st into top of beg ch-3 to join.

Round 3: ch3 (counts as first dc), 1dc into next st, *[1dc, ch1, 1dc] into ch-1 sp, 1dc into each of next 3 sts; rep from * 4 times more, [1dc, ch1, 1dc] into ch-1 sp, 1dc into next st, sl st into top of beg ch-3 to join.

Round 4: ch2 (counts as first hdc), 1hdc into each of next 2 sts, *[1hdc, ch1, 1hdc] into ch-1 sp, 1hdc into each of next 5 sts; rep from * 4 times more, [1hdc, ch1, 1hdc] into ch-1 sp, 1hdc into each of next 2 sts.
Fasten off, leaving a tail long enough to use for joining hexagons, and make an invisible join.
Repeat, making 13 hexagons in total: 5 CCa; 4 CCb; 4 CCc.

FINISHING

Weave in loose ends.

To join the hexagons, use whipstitch to sew the hexagons together through the back loops only of the outer edge stitches. This project has been designed to allow you to add hexagons to your rug as you see fit, they can be added in any direction and in any pattern you choose.

Feel-good tip

Enjoy the ongoing nature of this project. You will know when the process is complete—it will come to a natural end. As you return to your design, change the colors and textures according to your mood and feelings of the moment. It will tell its unique story, your story.

Persevere

Designed to move you outside your comfort zone, this will give you a great sense of achievement and encourage you to explore new skills.

1 Begin this exercise when you feel positive and ready for a challenge. Choose a crochet pattern from the following pages and place it somewhere where you can follow it closely and comfortably.

2 Familiarize yourself with the instructions and visualize the stitch combinations. Take a look at the images and make a mental note of how your project will look.

3 Keep this image in mind as you begin to crochet. Concentrate fully on the task at hand and believe that the pattern will lead you safely to success. Trust in the symbols and words— they will guide you through.

4 Be aware of any doubts or fears but don't judge them—they are simply normal thoughts that arise with all new experiences. Continue to tell yourself that you can do this.

5 Note the structure of the stitch combinations. Check each pattern repeat and row as you go. If you make an error, return to it. Use it as an opportunity to learn. This is the best way of acquiring new skills. Feel a sense of success as you put it right.

6 Develop an ongoing sense of achievement as you complete each stitch, each row. You are moving forward toward your goal, one stitch at a time.

7 As you master the skills, your confidence will grow and you will begin to see the world anew.

8 Feel that boost of feel-good chemicals flush through you. It's the reward for your perseverance and patience. Congratulations!

Bold Bunting

This bunting is perfect for adding a playful pop of color to your home décor. Once you get the hang of your first motif, this gorgeous bunting will fly off your hook.

YOU WILL NEED

* DK-weight, wool/acrylic/cashmere blend yarns (approx. 1¾ oz/50 g; 137 yds/125 m)
CCa 2 balls in coral
CCb 1 ball in dark green
* Size 7 (4.5 mm) hook
* Yarn needle

GAUGE

17 sc and 16 rows measure 4" (10 cm).

DIMENSIONS

49" (124 cm) strand of Bunting.

Each Bunting Motif measures 7" (18 cm) wide and 4½" (11.5 cm) tall.

NOTES

* Adjust the length of your bunting by creating more, or fewer, motifs as required.
* One motif uses approximately 27 yds (24.5 m) of yarn, so you can mix and match the color of your bunting by changing the yarn for each motif.

TO MAKE A BUNTING MOTIF (MAKE 7 PER STRING)

Using CCa, ch4, sl st into first ch to form a ring.

Row 1: ch2 (counts as first sc), 7sc into ring, turn. (8 sts)

Row 2: ch2 (counts as first sc), 2sc blo into each of next 6 sts, 1sc blo into last st, turn. (14 sts)

Row 3: ch2 (counts as first sc), 1sc flo into each of next 13 sts to end of row, turn. (14 sts)

Row 4: ch3 (counts as first dc), 1dc blo into next st, *ch2, 1dc blo into each of next 2 sts; repeat from * 5 times more, turn. (14 sts)

Row 5: ch2 (counts as first sc), *work [2sc, ch1, 2sc] into next ch-2 sp; repeat from * 5 times more, 1sc into last st, turn. (26 sts)

Row 6: ch2 (counts as first sc), skip 2 sts, work [3sc, ch1, 3sc] into blo of next ch (the ch-1 from previous row), *skip 4 sts, work [3sc, ch1, 3sc] into blo of next st; rep from * 4 times more to last 3 sts, skip 2 sts, 1sc into last st, turn. (38 sts)

Row 7: ch2 (counts as first sc), ch4, skip 3 sts, sl st flo into next ch-1 from previous row, ch4, *skip 6 sts, sl st flo into ch-1 from previous row, ch4; rep from * 4 times more, skip 3 sts, 1sc into last st, turn.

Row 8: ch2 (counts as first sc), 4sc into next ch-4 sp, *ch2, 4sc into next ch-4 sp; rep from * 5 times more to last st, 1sc into last st, turn. (30 sts)

Row 9: ch2 (counts as first sc), 1sc flo into each of next 4 sts, *1sc flo into next ch, ch2, 1sc flo into next ch, 1sc flo into each of next 4 sts; rep from * 5 times more to last st, 1sc into last st, turn. (42 sts)

Row 10: ch3 (counts as first dc), skip 5 sts, [3dc, ch2, 3dc] into ch-2 sp from previous row, *skip 6 sts, [3dc, ch2, 3dc] into ch2 sp from previous row; rep from * 4 times more to last ch-2 sp, ch 3, skip 5 sts, sl st into last st. Do not turn.

Row 11: ch2 (counts as first sc), rotate to work along top edge of Bunting, 1sc into next ch-2 sp, 1sc around next sc, 2sc into next ch-2 sp,

Tip
Choose your yarn
carefully—cotton yarns
weigh more per yard
than acrylic yarns.

1sc around next sc, 1sc into next ch-2 sp, 1sc around next sc, 2sc into next ch-2 sp, 1sc around next sc, 1sc into next ch-2sp, 3sc into loop at center of motif, 1sc around next sc, 1sc into next ch-2 sp, 1sc around next sc, 2sc into next ch-3 sp, 1sc around next sc, 1sc into next ch-2 sp, 1sc around next sc, 2sc into next ch-2 sp, 1sc around next sc, 1sc into last ch-sp, turn. (27 sts along top)

Row 12: ch2 (counts as first sc), 1sc flo into each of next 26 sts, turn.

Row 13: ch2 (counts as first sc), 1sc into each of next 26 sts, turn.
Fasten off.

FINISHING

To block each motif, soak in tepid water and remove any excess water by rolling the motifs in a clean colorfast towel, taking care not to twist them. Lay the motifs flat to dry, reshaping and pinning if necessary.
Weave in the loose ends.

To make the bunting strand

To attach the bunting motifs together, using CCb, join yarn into the top right corner of the right-hand side of one bunting motif. Work 1sc blo into each st along the top of each bunting motif, moving from one motif to the next without breaking the yarn, to attach all seven motifs in a strand.

Feel-good tip

Take pride in hanging your bunting somewhere visible where it will attract positive feedback to reinforce your confidence. You have created a beautiful piece of work. It's time now to accept the compliments with a smile.

Vibrant Layered Necklace

Multiple strands of gold chain and brightly colored crocheted pieces are combined to create this stunning showstopper necklace. Try your hand at making both standard single crochet stitches and more intricate lacy motifs in this gorgeous pattern.

YOU WILL NEED

* Small amount of DK-weight, wool blend yarns in
CCa yellow
CCb white
CCc teal
CCd coral
* Size B-1 (2.25 mm) hook
* Seed beads
* Bead stringing thread
* Leather crimps
* Gold chain strands ranging from 18–30" (46–76 cm)
* Jump rings (assorted sizes)
* Double loop connectors or small split rings
* Necklace clasp(s)
* Yarn needle
* Jewelry crimping pliers
* Jewelry pliers, 2 pairs

GAUGE

36 sc and 24 rows measure 4" (10 cm) square in chevron pattern.

DIMENSIONS

* Chevron: 3½" (9 cm) square.
* Lacy Motif: 2½" (6.5 cm) high × 1½" (4 cm) wide.

TO MAKE THE CHEVRON MOTIF

Using CCa, ch37.

Row 1: ch2 (counts as first sc), 1sc into third ch from hook, 1sc into each of next 16 ch, skip 2 ch, 1sc into each of next 18 chs, turn. (36 sts) Fasten off CCa. Join in CCb.

Row 2: ch2 (counts as first sc), 1sc into base of beg ch-2, 1sc into next 16 sts, skip 2 sts, 1sc into each of next 16 sts, 2sc into last st, turn. (36 sts) Fasten off CCb. Join in CCc.

Row 3: repeat Row 2.
Fasten off CCc. Join in CCd.

Row 4: repeat Row 2.
Fasten off CCd. Join in CCa.

Row 5: repeat Row 2.
Fasten off CCa. Join in CCb.

Row 6: repeat Row 2.
Fasten off CCb. Join in CCc.

Row 7: repeat Row 2.
Fasten off CCc. Join in CCd.

Row 8: repeat Row 2.
Fasten off CCd. Join in CCb.

Row 9: repeat Row 2.
Fasten off.

TO MAKE A LACY MOTIF (MAKE 3)

Using CCa, ch10, sl st into first ch to form a ring, ch6, sl st into first ch to form a second ring.

Row 1: into ch-10 ring work [sl st, ch2, 3sc, 1dc, ch4, 1dc, ch4, 1dc, ch4, 1tr, ch5, 1tr, ch4, 1dc, ch4, 1dc, ch4, 1dc, 4sc]; 6sc into ch-6 ring, sl st into second ch of first ch-2 to join.
Fasten off.

FINISHING

To block each motif

Soak in tepid water and remove any excess water by rolling the motifs in a clean colorfast towel, taking care not to twist them. Lay the motifs flat to dry, reshaping and pinning if necessary. Once dry, weave in the loose ends.

To assemble the chevron necklace strand

Attach a jump ring to each upper corner of the chevron motif and thread a 10" (25 cm) strand of gold chain through each jump ring on each side of the chevron to form one necklace strand.

Tip

For a secure join, use one pair of pliers in each hand to ease open the jump rings sideways, the minimum distance required to attach the ring to the fabric, chain, or clasp. To close, use pliers to ease the open ends closed.

To assemble the bead and lacy motif necklace strand

Attach a jump ring and double loop connectors or a split ring to the top of each lacy motif. Cut a length of beading thread approximately 40" (1 m) long, make a short loop at one end and make a double-stranded slipknot. Place the loop and knot in a leather crimp so that the ends protrude beyond the base of the crimp but not the loop or knot. The base of the leather crimp is the end without the ring. Using crimping pliers, which have two notches in their jaws, flatten the leather crimp using the outer notch and then compress the leather crimp using the inner notch. Trim the short thread end. Thread a necklace strand with seed beads until it is approximately 32" (80 cm) long, make a double-stranded slipknot as close to the last bead as possible, place the loop and knot into a leather crimp and secure as before. Fold the beaded strand in half, attach the first lacy motif to the center of the beaded strand, and then attach a lacy motif equidistant, on either side of the central lacy motif.

To assemble the final necklace

Add extra strands of gold chains, at varying lengths, to achieve the desired effect. You can keep each strand as an individual necklace by adding a clasp to each one. Or, you can gather all the strands together, attach a single jump ring to each group of ends, and attach the two jump rings to a single clasp.

CARE INSTRUCTIONS

Do not wash the necklace as a whole. If the fabric pieces require cleaning, detach all metal from the pieces before washing. For best results gently hand-wash. Roll in a clean colorfast towel to squeeze out any excess water. Be sure to avoid twisting or wringing the piece. Re-block and lay flat to dry. Reassemble necklace.

Feel-good tip

Regular novelty experiences and the learning of new skills are essential for brain health. The mix of stitches in this project make for a good learning experience and a rewarding challenge.

Find Joy

Rhythmic, repetitive movements stimulate the release of serotonin to raise your mood. Enhance this effect with the following uplifting exercise. Practice it as you create your feel-good, happiness projects on the following pages.

1 Choose yarn colors that make you feel naturally happy. Their texture should feel so good and luxurious as they run through your fingers that you can't help but smile.

2 Settle into the rhythmic process of your hands, moving along to the crochet instructions, and smile as you recognize the familiar feeling of calm and well-being this brings.

3 Be aware of your body's chemistry changing and feel powerful in your ability to alter your emotions. Experience a sense of control and safety in this knowledge.

4 Let the problems of the world fade from your perspective. The past is no more. The future does not exist. You have no reason to be other than deeply content in this present moment.

5 Allow yourself to feel alive and untroubled.

6 As your mood improves it triggers more feel-good chemicals that cascade through your body. Feel them flooding your brain. Sense them reaching the very tips of your toes and fingers, to the very core of your being.

7 Think about spreading this happiness to others. Imagine giving your project as a gift—perhaps to a friend who needs cheering up, even a complete stranger. Imagine their surprised reaction and delight. Smile with them. Know you will make their day.

8 Remind yourself of the positive power and simple joy of creating and giving.

9 Be content in the knowledge that you can feel good whenever and wherever you choose to do so. You have that power at your fingertips.

Wake Up Happy Washcloths

Beautiful textured washcloths add a little luxury to your life.
Pamper yourself or a friend by making this easy pattern in a soft cotton yarn.

YOU WILL NEED

* Worsted-weight cotton, (approx. 1¾ oz/50 g; 93 yds/85 m)

* Plain Washcloth:
MC 1 ball in white or yellow

If adding a contrast edge:
CC small amount of yellow

* Striped Washcloth:
MC 1 ball in white
CC 1 ball in yellow

* Ripple Washcloth:
MC 1 ball in white
CC 1 ball in yellow

* Size H-8 (5 mm) hook

* Yarn needle

GAUGE

* Plain and Striped Washcloth: 6 blocks measure 4½" (11.5 cm) and 11 rows measure 4" (10 cm) over block stitch.

* Ripple Stitch Washcloth: 21 sts (2 repeats) measure 4¾" (12 cm) and 7 rows measure 4" (10 cm) over ripple stitch.

DIMENSIONS

8" (20 cm) square.

NOTE

Each plain washcloth uses approximately 65 yds (60 m) of yarn (¾ ball of recommended yarn).

TO MAKE A PLAIN CLOTH

Using MC or color of choice, ch30.

Row 1: skip 2 ch (counts as 1sc), work [1hdc, 1dc] into next ch, *skip 2 ch, work [1sc, 1hdc, 1dc] into next ch; rep from * to last 3 ch, skip 2 ch, 1sc into last ch, turn. (9 blocks)

Row 2: ch1 (counts as first sc), work [1hdc, 1dc] into sc at base of ch-1, *skip 2 sts, work [1sc, 1hdc, 1dc] into next sc; rep from * to last 3 sts, skip 2 sts, 1sc into last st (turning ch), turn.

Rows 3– 21: repeat Row 2.

Row 22: ch1 (counts as first sc), work [1hdc, 1dc] into next st, *skip 2 sts, work [1sc, 1hdc, 1dc] into next sc; repeat from * to last 3 sts, skip 2 sts, 1sc into last st (turning ch). Do not turn. For contrast edging, fasten off MC. Join in CC.

To make the edging:

Ch1, rotate to work along side edge, 2sc into next st, work evenly approximately 1sc into edge of each row; rotate to work along bottom edge, 2sc into corner, 1sc into each st; rotate to work along side edge, 2sc into corner, work evenly approximately 1sc into edge of each row; rotate to work along top edge, 2sc into corner, 1sc into each st, sl st into first sc to join. Fasten off. Weave in loose ends.

TO MAKE A STRIPED CLOTH

Using MC, ch30.

Row 1: skip 2 ch (counts as 1sc), work [1hdc, 1dc] into next ch, *skip 2 ch, work [1sc, 1hdc, 1dc] into next ch; rep from * to last 3 ch, skip 2 ch, 1sc into last ch, turn.

Row 2: ch1 (counts as first sc), work [1hdc, 1dc] into next st, *skip 2 sts, work [1sc, 1hdc, 1dc] into next sc; rep from * to last 3 sts, skip 2 sts, 1sc into last st (turning ch), joining in CC on the final stage of the st, turn.

Fasten off MC.

Rows 3–21: repeat Row 2, changing color every 2 rows, ending with MC.

Row 22: ch1 (counts as first sc), work [1hdc, 1dc] into next st, *skip 2 sts, work [1sc, 1hdc, 1dc] into next sc; rep from * to last 3 sts, skip 2 sts, 1sc into last st (turning ch). Do not turn. Fasten off MC. Join CC into corner near last st worked in MC.

To make the edging

Rotate to work along side edge, 2sc into next st, work evenly approximately 1sc into edge of each row; rotate to work along bottom edge, 2sc into corner, 1sc into each st; rotate to work along side edge, 2sc into corner, work evenly approximately 1sc into edge of each row; rotate to work along top edge, 2sc into corner, 1sc into each st, sl st into first sc to join.

Fasten off. Weave in loose ends.

TO MAKE A RIPPLE CLOTH

Using MC, ch28.

Row 1: 1dc into fourth ch from hook (counts as first and second dc), *1dc into each of next 2 ch, dc3tog over next 3 ch, 1dc into each of next 2 ch, 3dc into next ch; rep from * ending last repeat with 2dc into last ch, joining in CC on the final stage of the last st, turn.

Row 2: ch3 (counts as first dc), 1dc into base of beg ch-3, *1dc into each of next 2 sts, dc3tog over next 3 sts, 1dc into each of next 2 sts, 3dc into next st; rep from * ending last rep with 2dc into last st (turning chain) joining in MC on final stage of last st, turn.

Rows 3–13: repeat Row 2, changing color every row, ending with MC.

Fasten off MC. Join CC into corner near last st worked in MC.

To make the edging

Rotate to work along side edge, 2sc into next st, 2sc into edge of each row; rotate to work along bottom edge, 2sc into corner, 1sc into each st; rotate to work along side edge, 2sc into corner, 2sc into edge of each row; rotate to work along top edge, 2sc into corner, 1sc into each st, sl st into first sc to join.

Fasten off. Weave in loose ends.

Feel-good tip

Each of us has the power to change our body chemistry. Use your bright washcloth every morning and evening, and as you do so recall and immerse yourself in your feelings of joy.

Tip
Think carefully about
the fiber you choose—soft
unmercerized cottons are
good for absorbency and
linen is best for exfoliation.
Environmentally friendly
cottons and linens are an
added benefit.

Spread the Love Hairclips

Make these delicate crochet flowers in soft cotton and enjoy its texture.
Discover the big impact of small flowers on your mood. Give a
flower to your friends and watch them smile, too!

YOU WILL NEED

* Scraps of Sport-weight, cotton yarns in
CCa yellow
CCb dark pink
CCc cream
CCd pale teal
CCe lime green
CCf pink
CCg light pink
CCh mustard
* Size D-3 (3.25 mm) hook
* Yarn needle
* Cotton embroidery thread in yellow (optional)
* Bobby Pin findings with flat pads
* Small amount of felt for backing flowers
* Glue gun
* PVA glue

GAUGE

Gauge is not important in this project

DIMENSIONS

Flowers range from 2–2½" (5–6.5 cm) in diameter.

SPECIAL STITCHES

SPSL spike slip stitch: insert hook into sl st on Round 2, yrh, draw up a loop to the same height as the working row, and draw through both loops on hook.

TO MAKE A SIX-PETAL FLOWER

Uses three shades of yarn.
Using CCe or color of choice, make a magic ring.
Round 1: ch1, 6sc into ring, sl st to first sc to join.
Fasten off CCe. Join in CCb into any st.
Round 2: [ch8, sl st into next sc] 6 times, sl st into first sl st to join. (6 ch-8 loops)
Round 3: *work [2sc, 2hdc, 5dc, 2hdc, 2sc] into next ch-8 loop; rep from * 5 times more, sl st to first sc to join. (6 petals)
Fasten off CCb. Join in CCh into third st of any petal.
Round 4: ch1, 1sc into base of beg ch-1, 1sc into next st, 1hdc into each of next 2 sts, 2hdc into next st, 1hdc into each of next 2 sts, 1sc into each of next 4 sts, SPSL, skip next 2 sts, *1sc into each of next 2 sts, 1hdc into each of next 2 sts, 2hdc into next st, 1hdc

into each of next 2 sts, 1sc into each of next 4 sts, SPSL, skip next 2 sts; rep from * 4 times more, sl st to first sc to join.
Fasten off and weave in loose ends.

FINISHING

Cut a small circle of felt, attach to the back of the flower, and glue in place. Glue a bobby pin to the felt circle and leave to dry.

TO MAKE A DAISY

Uses two shades of yarn.
Using CCb or color of choice, ch4, sl st to first ch to form a ring.
Round 1: ch1, 10sc into ring, sl st to first sc to join. (10 sts)
Fasten off CCb. Join in CCc into front loop only of any st.
Round 2: working into flo, [ch6, 1sc into third ch from hook, 1hdc into each of next 2 ch, 1sc into last ch, sl st into front loop of next st] 10 times, ending with a sl st to first st to join. (10 petals)
Round 3: working behind petals on Round 2, working into blo, sl st to back loop of first petal, [ch7, 1sc into third ch from hook, 1hdc into

Tip

Instead of a bobby pin, you could attach a safety pin to the back of your flower to make a brooch. Alternatively, leave off the bobby pin and simply place your crochet flowers around your home or office.

each of next 3 ch, 1sc into last ch, sl st into back loop of next st] 10 times, ending with a sl st to first st. (10 petals)

Fasten off and weave in loose ends.

FINISHING

Cut a small circle of felt, place it on the back of the flower, and glue in place. Glue a bobby pin to the felt circle and leave to dry.

TO MAKE A CLUSTER OF FLOWERS (MAKE 3)

Using CCa or color of choice, make a magic ring.

Round 1: ch1, 5sc into ring, sl st to first sc to join. (5 sts)

Fasten off CCa. Join in CCb, CCd or color of choice into any st.

Round 2: *work [sl st, ch4, 3tr, ch4, sl st] into next st; rep from * 4 times more, ending with sl st into first sl st.

Fasten off.

Make three of these pretty flowers using a different yarn shade for Round 2 in each case.

To make the leaf (make 1)

Using CCe, ch7.

Round 1: 1sc into second ch from hook, 1hdc into next ch, 1dc into each of next 3 ch, work [2hdc, ch2, 1sc into the back of the second ch from hook, 2hdc] into last st; rotate to work along the other side of ch, 1dc into each of next 3 sts, 1hdc into next st, 1sc into last st, sl st to first sc to join.

Fasten off and weave in loose ends.

FINISHING

Pin the three flowers together in a neat cluster, add a leaf pointing outward underneath. Take a small circle of felt, place it under the flower and leaf cluster, and glue in place. Glue a bobby pin to the felt circle and leave to dry.

TO MAKE A CAMELLIA FLOWER

Uses two shades of yarn.

Using CCg or color of choice, make a magic ring.

Round 1: ch4 (counts as first dc and 1 ch), work [1 dc, ch1] into ring 5 times, sl st to third ch of beg ch-4 to join. (6 dc and 6 ch-1 sp)

Round 2: [ch4, skip 1 dc, sl st into next dc] 3 times, sl st into base of beg ch-4 to join. (3 ch-4 sp)

Round 3: sl st into first ch-4 sp, *work [ch2, 5dc, ch2, sl st] into same ch-4 sp, sl st into next ch-4 loop; rep from * twice more. (3 petals)

Round 4: folding petals forward and working into back of next petal, ch2, *sl st to base of dc at center of petal, ch5; rep from * twice more, sl st into first ch-5 loop. (3 ch-5 sp)

Round 5: *work [ch2, 6dc, ch2, sl st] into next ch-5 sp, sl st into next ch-5 sp; rep from * twice more. (3 petals)

Fasten off CCg. Join in CCb.

Round 6: fold petals forward and working into back of a petal from Round 5, repeat Round 4.

Round 7: *work [ch1, 1hdc, 6dc, 1hdc, ch1, sl st] into next ch-5 sp, sl st into next ch-5 sp; rep from * twice more. (3 petals)

Fasten off and weave in loose ends.

To make the leaf (make 1)

Using CCe, work as for Daisy.

FINISHING

To make the stamens

Cut 3 lengths of yellow yarn or embroidery cotton, approximately 3" (7.5 cm) long. Make a knot in each end. Dip each length in PVA glue, remove the excess and leave to dry. When the stamens are dry, fold in half and gently pull folded end through center of flower using a crochet hook. Secure at back with a stitch.

Cut a small circle of felt, place it on the back of the flower and leaf, and glue in place. Glue a bobby pin to the felt circle and leave to dry.

Feel-good tip

Place these bright and cheerful flowers around your home and office as a reminder to smile. Share some happiness with others too, by giving the beautiful flower clips as gifts.

Friendship

The projects on pages 104–107 have been designed especially for crocheting with others. Take them to your crochet circle and celebrate being part of a supportive community.

1 Join your group and notice others as they arrive and settle into the gathering community. You will soon become a cohesive circle creating, laughing, and sharing together.

2 If you are new to the group, use the quiet rhythm of your movements to calm any anxious emotions. They are normal. They will pass.

3 Notice the uniqueness of each member. Celebrate the differences between you and revel in the opportunity to spend your time with such a diverse group of people.

4 Make an effort to learn from and share with each person in the group. It's a new opportunity every time you meet.

5 Feel a deep sense of belonging and support in sharing with, and learning from, each other. These new experiences will extend your knowledge and perception of the world.

6 As you all relax, an easy chatter and laughter emerges. It is the hallmark of your group. Others in the vicinity look on with a wistful desire to join in too. Invite them in.

7 When quiet, creative moments occur, enjoy the feeling of silent connection. Learn to "just be" in the company of others.

8 You have the choice to make eye contact or not. When you feel the need, simply sit and crochet quietly, safe in the knowledge that everyone there understands. Know deep in your heart you belong.

9 As you part company, begin to look forward to the next time you will meet.

Friendship Quilt

Ask each friend to create one large flower in their favorite colors. Work together to make lots of small flowers to link your individual creative selves in a timeless quilt that can be added to at any time.

YOU WILL NEED

* Worsted-weight wool blend yarn, (approx. 1¾ oz/50 g; 98 yds/90 m), 2 balls each in MC yellow CCa pink CCb light pink CCc blue CCd green CCe maroon

* Size H-8 (5 mm) hook

* Yarn needle

GAUGE

Gauge is not important in this project.

DIMENSIONS

Approximately 20" (51 cm) square.*

*The quilt can be added to at any time, and can be made to any desired size.

TO MAKE A LARGE FLOWER

Using MC, ch4, sl st into first ch to form a ring.

Round 1: ch1, 12sc into ring, sl st into first sc to join. (12 sts)

Round 2: ch3 (counts as first dc), 1dc into base of beg ch-3, 2dc into each st to end of round, sl st into top of beg ch-3 to join. (24 sts)
Fasten off MC. Join in CC of choice.

Round 3: *ch3, [yrh, insert hook into same st, yrh, pull up a loop as tall as the ch-3] 3 times, into next st [yrh, insert hook, yrh, pull up a loop as tall as the ch-3] 3 times, yrh and draw through all 13 loops on hook, ch2, sl st into next st; rep from * 11 times more. (12 puff-petals)
Fasten off and weave in loose ends.

TO MAKE A SMALL FLOWER

Using MC, ch4, sl st into first ch to form a ring.

Round 1: ch1, 12sc into ring, sl st into first sc to join. (12 sts)
Fasten off MC. Join in CC of choice.

Round 2: *ch3, [yrh, insert hook into same st, yrh, pull up a loop as tall as the ch-3] 3 times, into next st [yrh, insert hook, yrh, pull up a loop as tall as the ch-3] 3 times, yrh and draw through all 13 loops on hook, ch2, sl st into next st; rep from * 5 times more. (6 puff-petals)
Fasten off and weave in loose ends.

FINISHING

To assemble the quilt

Lay flowers face down and position them so that they fit together nicely. Using one of the CC colors from the flowers you are joining, loop a short length of yarn around the ch-2 or ch-3 of each adjacent petal and tie them together with a knot. Trim the ends to approximately ½" (12 mm). Repeat this around every petal.

Feel-good tip

Why not create this with your crochet friends? Get together to make the individual flowers then knot them together as a symbol of your friendship.

Let's Be Friends Bracelets

These easy bracelets can be made with friends and worn to remind you that you belong together. The pattern can be made with or without the beads.

YOU WILL NEED

* Scraps of pearlized cotton embroidery thread, size 5, 2 yds (2 m) in light blue, dark blue, light green, medium green, dark green, yellow, and golden yellow
* Size E-4 (3.5 mm) hook
* Glass beads, size 6, 30 beads (optional)
* Wooden bead, ¼" (6 mm)
* A needle that will fit through the beads

GAUGE

Gauge is not important in this project.

DIMENSIONS

7" (18 cm) bracelet.

NOTE

If you require a larger or smaller bracelet, simply add or subtract stitches to the foundation chain.

TO MAKE A FRIENDSHIP BRACELET

Using color of choice and leaving a 6" (15 cm) tail, ch46.

Row 1: working through top loop throughout, sl st into sixth ch from hook, sl st into each st to end of ch.

Fasten off leaving a 6" (15 cm) tail. Do not weave in ends.

TO MAKE A BEADED FRIENDSHIP BRACELET

If making a beaded bracelet, thread 30 beads onto embroidery thread.

Using the color of choice and leaving a 6" (15 cm) tail, ch46.

Row 1: working through top loop throughout, sl st into sixth ch from hook, sl st into each of next 5 ch, [slide one bead along the thread to the base of the working loop on the hook, sl st into next ch] 30 times, sl st into each of last 5 ch. Fasten off leaving a 6" (15 cm) tail. Do not weave in ends.

FINISHING

With the starting tail and ending tail held together, make a double overhand knot at the base of the bracelet. Thread the wooden bead onto the tail and slide up to the knot. Make another double overhand knot directly below the wooden bead to secure it in place. Trim the thread ends.

Feel-good tip

Enjoy the simplicity of these projects. Between meetings they will remind you of your supportive crochet community. Focus on these feelings of belonging when you feel alone. Let these bracelets remind you to make a date with your friends.

Chapter 3
Techniques

Tools and Materials

Making a beautiful finished project starts with choosing the right tools and materials. Taking a bit of time to consider the possibilities before you begin will pay dividends in the end.

HOOK SIZES

All the projects in this book use hooks smaller than size N/P-15 (10 mm). Recommended hook sizes are specified at the start of each pattern. The chart below lists the hook sizes required for the patterns in this book.

US Size	Millimeter
B-1	(2.25 mm)
D-3	(3.25 mm)
E-4	(3.5 mm)
G-6	(4 mm)
7	(4.5 mm)
H-8	(5 mm)
M/N-13	(9 mm)
N/P-15	(10 mm)

CHOOSING YOUR YARN

Before you start each project, you will need to decide what type of fiber you would like to use: animal, plant, or synthetic. Each type of fiber has its own characteristics. Wool (animal), for instance, is warm and absorbent, but requires careful washing and drying. Cotton, bamboo, hemp, and linen (plant) are light-weight, require less careful washing, and work well for warm-weather garments. Synthetic fibers such as acrylic and polyester are the cheapest of the yarn options and are machine washable—making them the most popular choice for beginners. These fibers or blends of these fibers are spun to create yarn.

Yarn can be spun to different weights (thicknesses) and the names for these weights will differ from country to country. To ensure that you are using the correct weight, check the details of the recommended yarn for the project (see pages 140–141) and compare it to the yarn you are planning to substitute. Use the chart opposite to confirm your choice of yarn is the same weight as the recommended yarn. Working a gauge swatch is always a good idea.

CROCHET HOOKS

Crochet hooks are made from many different materials, in various shapes, and sizes. Depending on the grip (see Holding the Hook, page 112), you might find one design more comfortable than another. Ergonomic hooks, for example, are great for people who are prone to wrist pain. In addition, it is useful to remember that some hooks work better with particular yarns or fibers: wooden hooks work well with slippery yarns such as silk, but not so well with acrylics or wool; hooks with relatively blunt tips are useful if working with yarn that splits easily.

OTHER TOOLS

There are a number of other tools that you will find useful:

* A small pair of scissors with pointed tips for cutting yarn ends close to the work. Take care that you do not accidentally cut your work!
* A yarn needle or a blunt tapestry needle with a large eye for weaving in a yarn tail. A blunt needle will slide between the strands of the yarn rather than through them, which could weaken the fiber.

YARN WEIGHTS

Yarn-Weight Symbol and Category Name	⬤1 Super Fine	⬤2 Fine	⬤3 Light	⬤4 Medium	⬤5 Bulky	⬤6 Super Bulky
Types of Yarn in Category	Sock, Fingering, Baby	Sport, Baby	DK, Light Worsted	Worsted, Afghan, Aran	Chunky, Craft, Rug	Bulky, Roving
Crochet Gauge Ranges* in Single Crochet to 4" (10 cm)	21 to 32 sts	16 to 20 sts	12 to 17sts	11 to 14 sts	8 to 11sts	5 to 9 sts
Recommended Hook in Metric Size Range	2.25 to 3.5 mm	3.5 to 4.5 mm	4.5 to 5.5 mm	5.5 to 6.5 mm	6.5 to 9 mm	9 mm and larger
Recommended Hook in US Size Range	B-1 to E-4	E-4 to 7	7 to I-9	I-9 to K-10½	K-10½ to M-13	M-13 and larger

These are guidelines only. The above reflect the most commonly used gauges and needle or hook sizes for specific yarn categories.

✳ Stitch markers are useful for a number of reasons. They can be used to mark the start of a round, or to mark the start of individual repeats within a round. Not only can they save you a lot of counting, but they can also save you a lot of frogging (ripping out). If you do not have any stitch markers, use a piece of scrap yarn to mark the stitches instead.

✳ A ruler for measuring gauge swatches and a tape measure will also be useful.

✳ Rust proof pins with large heads are useful when sewing motifs together.

OPTIONAL TOOLS

Occasionally you will be required to sew fabric to the back of a piece of crochet or add a lining. In each case, the fabric may be hand or machine sewn. Likewise, the Vibrant Layered Necklace, page 89, recommends specialist beading and jewelry-making tools for the best results. Read the pattern requirements carefully and ensure at the start of each new project you have everything you need and feel confident about the finishing requirements.

Why not start with a simple project first, like the Calming Mandalas on page 28?

Getting Started

Start every project by reviewing what you are going to do and how you are going to do it. Prepare your mind for the journey. It is always a good idea to look through the stitches and techniques you will need, even if you have a lot of crochet experience.

HOLDING THE HOOK

People generally hold their hook in one of two ways: the knife hold or the pencil hold. You can use whichever method you find most comfortable. You should hold the hook in your dominant hand, while the non-dominant hand holds the yarn and controls the tension.

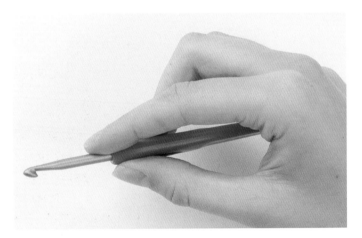

Knife Hold

Hold the hook as you would hold your knife when you are eating. Most hooks have a flat surface called a thumb-rest. The tip of the thumb should be pressed flat against this thumb-rest. The forefinger should rest lightly on the back of the hook.

Pencil Hold

With the thumb resting on the thumb-rest, hold the hook as if it is a pencil and you are trying to write with it. The tip of the forefinger should be supporting the back of the hook.

HOLDING THE YARN

There are many different ways to hold the yarn. We will look at the two main options: woven and forefinger.

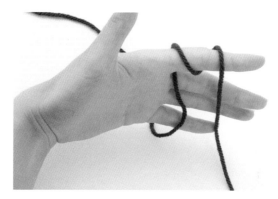

Woven Hold

Weave the yarn through the fingers as follows: over the forefinger, under the middle finger, and over the ring finger. If this feels too loose, wrap the yarn around the little finger once, like a ring.

Forefinger Hold

Wrap the yarn around the forefinger twice.

GAUGE

For many of the projects in this book, the gauge doesn't matter because the projects do not need to fit any particular size. For some projects, however, the crochet fabric will need to be made with a tight tension—for example, in projects like pillows that are stuffed. For these projects it might be useful to work a gauge swatch first to check the appearance and density of your crochet fabric. If you find that using the specified hook creates a fabric that is too open, use a smaller hook size. If the fabric is too tight, use a larger hook size.

Some patterns do suggest a particular gauge. This means a set number of stitches need to fit within a particular measurement. For example: 3 shells (18 sts) measure 4" (10 cm) and 6 shells (12 rows) measure 4¼" (10.5 cm) over pattern, using size H-8 (5 mm) hook.

However, everyone hooks with a different tension, and so a different hook may have to be used in order to achieve the right gauge. To check your gauge, crochet a 6" (15 cm) square using the hook size, yarn, and stitch (in this example, a shell stitch) stated in the pattern. Place a ruler horizontally across a row of stitches in the center of the square and insert pins 4" (10 cm) apart. Then count the stitches between the pins—including any partial stitches. For this example do you have 3 shells (18 sts)? If you have too many stitches, work a second square using a hook one size larger. If you have too few stitches, use a hook one size smaller. Keep making squares until you have the correct number of stitches between your markers. Check the vertical gauge in the same way, counting the number of rows between the pins—including any partial rows—and adjust the hook size as necessary.

Stitches

The following pages describe the basic crochet stitches you will need for the projects in this book. Take time to familiarize yourself with the stitches you will need before starting a new project—even if you are an experienced crocheter, a refresher is always useful.

SLIPKNOT

Place the end of the yarn in the left palm (right if you are left-handed) and hold it in place with the little finger and ring finger. Wrap the yarn clockwise around the forefinger so that the working yarn crosses over the tail of yarn and forms a loop. Insert the hook into the loop, catch the working yarn with the hook, and pull it through the loop. Hold both ends of yarn and pull them tight, but not too tight, until the slipknot rests comfortably around the hook. Unless you are specifically instructed to start with a magic ring, you will start all the crochet projects with a slipknot.

CHAIN STITCH (CH)

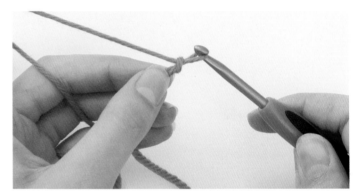

I With a slipknot already on the hook, hold the slipknot between the thumb and middle finger. Wrap the yarn around the hook by swinging the hook from front to back under the working yarn so that the working yarn forms a loop over the hook. This is known as a "yarn-over" or "yarn around hook." Still pinching the slipknot between thumb and forefinger, pull the slipknot slightly away from the hook.

2 Draw the loop created by the yarn-over through the loop that is already on the hook. Ensure that the hook is pointing downward as it gets closer to the loop on the hook, otherwise it will catch on the loop that is already on the hook. The first chain stitch is complete. Repeat until the required number of chain stitches have been worked. (The loop on the hook does not count as a stitch.)

ADDING TO THE FOUNDATION CHAIN

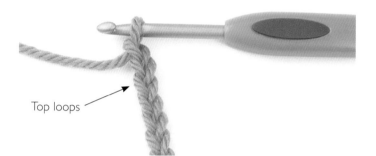

Top loops

Have a look at the foundation chain above. Can you see that each chain stitch forms a little "V"? When you work into the foundation chain to start the next row, you will be inserting the hook into the top loop only of each "V."

On the reverse side of the foundation chain there are a series of small bumps—one bump for each chain. Some patterns suggest you work into the back bumps rather than the V-shaped loops described above. Working into these back bumps means that the V-shaped loops are along the exposed edge, mimicking the top of the last row of stitches. Some find this edge more aesthetically pleasing and easier to seam, but it can be slightly more fiddly to work.

BEGINNING OR TURNING CHAINS

Beginning or turning chains are used to bring the start of a row or round and hook up to the height necessary to work the rest of the row or round. When the work is turned at the start of rows or rounds, the chain stitches at the start of the row or round are sometimes called a "turning chain." Not all patterns require the work to be turned, so in this book, the term "beginning chain" has been used to describe the chain at the beginning of a row or round—beg ch-3. The beginning chain usually replaces the first stitch, but not always.

Here is a general guide:

Slip stitches do not require a beginning chain as they do not add any height to a row or round.

Single crochet stitches require one beginning chain, but it is not often counted as a stitch.

Half double crochet stitches require two beginning chains. These two chains may be counted as the first stitch.

Double crochet stitches require three beginning chains. These three chains may be counted as the first stitch.

Treble crochet stitches require four beginning chains. These four chains may be counted as the first stitch.

The pattern will indicate if the beginning chain is counted as a stitch.

SLIP STITCH (SL ST)

Slip stitches do not add any height to the work. They are usually used to join rounds. They can also be used to join two pieces of crochet fabric together (instead of sewing them together) or to reinforce an edge.

Making a sl st into the foundation chain

I Insert the hook into top loop only of the second chain from the hook or the placement indicated in the pattern.

2 Wrap the yarn around the hook. Draw the yarn through both loops on the hook.

Making a sl st in subsequent rows/rounds

Insert the hook into the placement indicated in the pattern. Wrap the yarn around the hook and draw the yarn through both loops on the hook.

SINGLE CROCHET (SC)

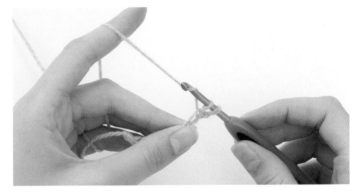

I Insert the hook into the top loop only of the second chain from the hook or the placement indicated in the pattern.

2 Wrap the yarn around the hook by swinging the hook from front to back under the working yarn.

3 Draw the yarn through the crochet fabric. There should now be two loops on the hook. (see above)

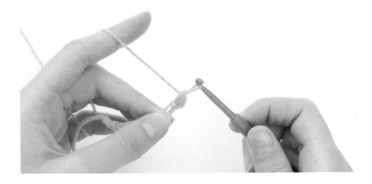

4 Wrap the yarn around the hook and draw the yarn through both loops on the hook to complete the single crochet stitch.

5 To work the next single crochet stitch, insert the hook into the next indicated stitch, and repeat Steps 2–4. Repeat until all the stitches indicated in the pattern have been worked.

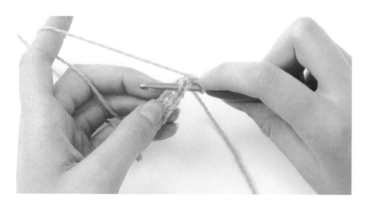

6 To work the next row, turn the work and crochet one (beginning) chain. The beginning chain doesn't count as a stitch. Insert the hook under both top loops of the first stitch, or into the placement indicated in the pattern, and repeat Steps 2–4. Repeat for each stitch as indicated in the pattern. The last single crochet stitch in a row should be worked in the first single crochet stitch of the previous row. Do not work into the beginning chain unless specified.

HALF DOUBLE CROCHET (HDC)

1 Wrap the yarn around the hook and insert the hook into the top loop only of the third chain from the hook or the placement indicated in the pattern.

4 Wrap the yarn around the hook and draw the yarn through all three loops on the hook to complete the half double crochet stitch.

2 Wrap the yarn around the hook again.
3 Draw the yarn through the crochet fabric. There should now be three loops on the hook. (see above)

5 To work the next half double crochet stitch, wrap the yarn around the hook, insert the hook into the next indicated stitch, and repeat Steps 2–4. Repeat until all the stitches indicated in the pattern have been worked.

6 To work the next row, turn the work and crochet two (beginning) chains. The beginning chain may count as the first half double crochet stitch of the row. Wrap the yarn around the hook, insert the hook under both loops of the second stitch or into the placement indicated in the pattern, and repeat Steps 2–4. Repeat for each stitch as indicated in the pattern. The last half double crochet stitch in the row should be worked in the second chain of the chain-2 beginning chain at the start of the previous row or the stitch indicated in the pattern.

Note on HDC: Occasionally a designer won't count the chain-2 (ch-2) beginning chain as a stitch. In which case, the first stitch is worked into the top loops of the first stitch at the base of the beginning chain, and the last stitch will fall in the last half double crochet stitch, not into the top of the ch-2 beginning chain. To avoid confusion, follow the pattern instructions and ensure that the stitch count tallies with the stitch count provided at the end of each row or round.

DOUBLE CROCHET (DC)

1 Wrap the yarn around the hook and insert the hook into the top loop only of the fourth chain from the hook or the placement indicated in the pattern.

2 Wrap the yarn around the hook again.
3 Draw the yarn through the crochet fabric. There should now be three loops on the hook. (see above)

(continues on next page)

4 Wrap the yarn around the hook and draw the yarn through the first two loops on the hook. There should now be two loops remaining on the hook.

6 To work the next double crochet stitch, wrap the yarn around the hook, insert the hook into the next indicated stitch, and repeat Steps 2–5. Repeat until all the stitches indicated in the pattern have been worked.

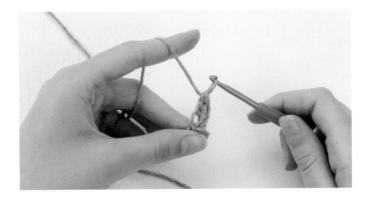

5 Wrap the yarn around the hook and draw the yarn through both remaining loops on the hook to complete the first double crochet stitch.

7 To work the next row, turn the work and crochet three (beginning) chains. The beginning chains may count as the first double crochet in the row—if so, this will be indicated in the pattern. Wrap the yarn around the hook and insert the hook under both loops of the second stitch or into the placement indicated in the pattern, and repeat Steps 2–5. Repeat for each stitch as indicated in the pattern. The last double crochet stitch of the row should be worked in the third chain of the chain-3 beginning chain at the start of the previous row or the stitch indicated in the pattern.

TREBLE CROCHET (TR)

1 Wrap the yarn around the hook twice and insert the hook into the top loop only of the fifth chain from the hook or the placement indicated in the pattern.

2 Wrap the yarn around the hook and draw the yarn through the crochet fabric. There should now be four loops on the hook. (see above)

3 Wrap the yarn around the hook and draw the yarn through the first two loops on the hook. Repeat three times to complete the first treble crochet stitch.

4 To work the next treble crochet stitch, wrap the yarn around the hook twice, insert the hook into the next indicated stitch, and repeat Steps 2–3. Repeat until all the stitches indicated in the pattern have been worked.

5 To work the next row, turn the work and crochet four (beginning) chains. The beginning chain may count as the first treble crochet in the row, the pattern will specify if so. Wrap the yarn around the hook twice and insert the hook under both loops of the second stitch or as indicated in the pattern, and repeat Steps 2–3. Repeat for each stitch as instructed. The last treble crochet stitch of the row should be worked in the fourth chain of the chain-4 beginning chain at the start of the previous row or the stitch indicated in the pattern.

Increasing and Decreasing

Crochet fabric is shaped by strategically increasing and decreasing the number of stitches in a row or round. The placement of these increases and decreases (and the necessary calculations) have been made by the project designer, but usually they follow a predictable pattern, which may be anticipated on following rows or rounds.

INCREASING

Whether you are using single crochet, half double crochet, double crochet, or treble crochet, the method for increasing the number of stitches remains the same.

To increase by one stitch

To increase by one stitch at the beginning, middle, or end of a row or round, simply work two stitches into the same stitch or position.

To increase more than one stitch

To increase by more than one stitch, work more than one stitch into the same stitch or position.

DECREASING

The number of stitches on a row or round may be reduced by either skipping a stitch or space or by working stitches together.

SINGLE CROCHET TWO STITCHES TOGETHER (SC2TOG)

1 Insert the hook into the indicated stitch or space, wrap the yarn around the hook, and draw the yarn through the crochet fabric. Insert the hook into the next indicated stitch or space, wrap the yarn around the hook, and draw the yarn through the crochet fabric—three loops are now on the hook. (see above)
2 Wrap the yarn around the hook and draw the yarn through all three loops on the hook.

HALF DOUBLE CROCHET TWO STITCHES TOGETHER (HDC2TOG)

1 Wrap the yarn around the hook and insert the hook into the indicated stitch or space. Wrap the yarn around the hook and draw the yarn through the crochet fabric. Wrap the yarn around the hook again, insert the hook into the next indicated stitch or space, wrap the yarn around the hook, and draw the yarn through the crochet fabric—five loops are now on the hook.

2 Wrap the yarn around the hook and draw the yarn through all five loops on the hook.

DOUBLE CROCHET TWO STITCHES TOGETHER (DC2TOG)

1 Wrap the yarn around the hook and insert the hook into the indicated stitch or space. Wrap the yarn around the hook and draw the yarn through the crochet fabric. Wrap the yarn around the hook again and draw the yarn through the first two loops on the hook—two loops now remain on the hook.

2 Wrap the yarn around the hook and insert the hook into the next indicated stitch or space, wrap the yarn around the hook, and draw the yarn through the crochet fabric—four loops are now on the hook. Wrap the yarn around the hook and draw the yarn through the first two loops on the hook—three loops now remain on the hook. (see above)

3 Wrap the yarn around the hook and draw the yarn through all three loops on the hook.

DOUBLE CROCHET THREE STITCHES TOGETHER (DC3TOG)

1 Wrap the yarn around the hook and insert the hook into the indicated stitch or space. Wrap the yarn around the hook and draw the yarn through the crochet. Wrap the yarn around the hook again and draw the yarn through the first two loops on the hook—two loops now remain on the hook.

2 Wrap the yarn around the hook and insert the hook into the next indicated stitch or space, wrap the yarn around the hook, and draw the yarn through the crochet fabric—four loops are now on the hook. Wrap the yarn around the hook and draw the yarn through the first two loops on the hook—three loops now remain on the hook. (see above)

3 Wrap the yarn around the hook and insert the hook into the next indicated stitch or space, wrap the yarn around the hook, and draw the yarn through the crochet fabric—five loops are now on the hook. Wrap the yarn around the hook and draw the yarn through the first two loops on the hook—four loops now remain on the hook.

4 Wrap the yarn around the hook and draw the yarn through all four loops on the hook.

TREBLE CROCHET TWO STITCHES TOGETHER (TR2TOG)

1 Wrap the yarn around the hook twice and insert the hook into the indicated stitch or space, wrap the yarn around the hook, and draw the yarn through the crochet.

2 Wrap the yarn around the hook and draw the yarn through the first two loops on the hook, twice—two loops now remain on the hook. Wrap the yarn around the hook twice and insert the hook into the next indicated stitch or space, wrap the yarn around the hook, and draw the yarn through the crochet. Wrap the yarn around the hook and draw the yarn through the first two loops on the hook, twice—three loops now remain on the hook.

3 Wrap the yarn around the hook and draw the yarn through all three loops on the hook. (see above)

Special Stitches

These stitches are variations on the stitches outlined on pages 114–121. They are not more difficult, they just require a bit more thought and explanation.

FRONT AND BACK LOOP ONLY STITCHES

As with chain stitches, the top loop of each single crochet, half double crochet, double crochet, and treble crochet forms a "V" shape.

Front loop only stitches (flo)

Front loop only stitches (flo) are made by inserting the hook into the front loop only, not through both loops. The front loop will always be the one closest to you when as you work. (see above)

Back loop only stitches (blo)

Back loop only stitches (blo) are made by inserting the hook into the back loop only, not through both loops. The back loop will always be the one furthest from you when you work.

REVERSE SINGLE CROCHET STITCH (CRAB STITCH)

The reverse single crochet stitch (crab stitch) is worked in the same way as the single crochet stitch, except that you work backward in the opposite direction. It forms a rope-like stitch that is perfect for edgings.

1 Insert the hook into both loops of the first stitch to the right of the hook or the stitch or loop indicated in the pattern. Wrap the yarn around the hook, and draw the yarn through the crochet fabric. Wrap the yarn around the hook again and draw the yarn through both loops on the hook.

2 To work the next stitch, swing the hook under the hand, by twisting the wrist, and insert it into both loops of the stitch to the right, before the stitch just worked into.

3 Wrap the yarn around the hook and draw the yarn through both loops on the hook.

4 Repeat Steps 2–3 until all the stitches indicated in the pattern have been worked.

Beginning a Round

There are three different ways to start a round. These methods are interchangeable, so feel free to use whichever method you prefer. When substituting methods, ensure that the stitch count is correct at the end of the first round.

MAKING THE FIRST ROUND INTO A CHAIN

This is the easiest of the three methods. Start with a beginning chain to represent the first stitch and add one chain. For example, if the first round is double crochet, you will need four chains (beginning chain of 3 + 1 extra). The beginning chain will count as the first stitch. The extra stitch is the chain furthest from the hook and will form the center—all the other stitches for the round will be made into this center chain.

To use this method instead of pattern text
For example, when pattern text reads: "Using CCa, make a magic ring. Round 1: ch3 (counts as first dc), 11dc into ring. (12 sts)"
You can substitute the above method as follows to make a pattern with a single chain in the center: chain 4 stitches and work 11 double crochet stitches into the fourth chain from the hook. This will create a stitch count of 12 sts for the first round.

RING OF CHAINS

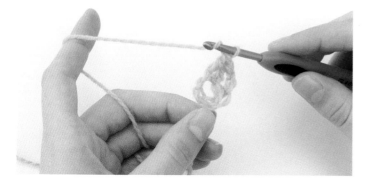

This method works well if the first round has a lot of stitches, as you can work a bigger ring of chains to accommodate them without bunching or overlapping. This method does leave a hole in the middle of the work, though, so if you want a tight center, use one of the other two methods.

Start with a short chain—usually half the number of stitches on the first round works well, but for a smaller center hole, a third of the stitches on the first round is usually long enough. Join this chain to form a ring by making a slip stitch into the chain farthest away from the hook. Work the required beginning chain for round 1, and then work the remainder of the round into the center of this ring.

To use this method instead of pattern text

For example, when pattern text reads: "Using CCa, make a magic ring. Round 1: ch3 (counts as first dc), 11dc into ring. (12 sts)" You can substitute the ring of chains method as follows: chain 6 stitches and sl st into first ch to form a ring. Chain 3 stitches and work 11 double crochet stitches into the center of the ring. This will create a stitch count of 12 sts for the first round.

Tip

When using the ring of chains method, work over the initial tail of yarn as the first round of stitches is worked. Once the round is complete, this tail of yarn may be pulled to close the central hole. Ensure that you weave this yarn tail securely to prevent the center from opening up again.

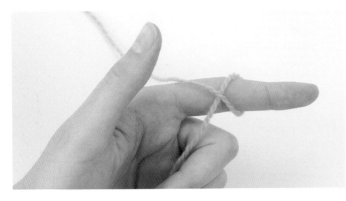

The magic ring can either yield a completely closed center, or accommodate as many stitches as you need.

1 Place the end of the yarn in the left palm (right if you are left-handed) and hold it in place with the little and ring finger. Wrap the yarn clockwise around the tip of the forefinger so that the working yarn crosses over the tail of yarn and forms a loop. (see above)

2 Use the thumb to hold the point where the two strands of yarn overlap. Ease the forefinger from the loop. Use the ring finger and little finger to tension the yarn.

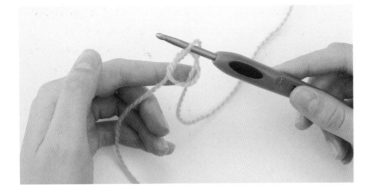

3 Insert the hook into the loop, catch the working tail of yarn with the hook, and pull it through the loop. (In the above image the ring is shown off the finger for clarity.)

4 Wrap the yarn around the hook and work a chain stitch. This chain stitch is not part of the beginning chain. It just secures the working yarn. Work the required beginning chains and then work the remainder of the round into the magic ring, remembering to work over the initial tail of yarn as well.

5 When the round is complete, close the hole by pulling on the initial tail of yarn. Weave in the initial tail of yarn securely. (see above)

To use this method instead of pattern text

For example, when pattern text reads: "Using MC, ch4, sl st into first ch to form a ring. Round 1: ch3 (counts as first dc), 11dc into ring, sl st into first dc to join. (12 sts)"

You can substitute the magic ring method as follows: work Steps 1–4, chain 3 and work 11 double crochet stitches into the magic ring.

This will create a stitch count of 12 stitches for the first round. Work Step 5.

Working in the Round

There are two main approaches to working a crochet fabric in the round: The last stitch of the round is either joined to the first stitch of the round and a new beginning chain is worked at the start of the next round, or work continues in a spiral and at the end of the round the stitches are not joined.

WORKING ROUNDS IN A SPIRAL

Mark each round with a stitch marker in the first or last stitch as directed in the pattern. Work as directed to the end of the round and check that the stitch count for the round is correct. Remove the stitch marker, work the first stitch of the next round into the previously marked stitch, and place the stitch marker into the stitch just worked. Continue until all the required rounds have been worked.

JOINING THE ROUND

Work as directed to the end of the round and check that the stitch count for the round is correct. The pattern will then indicate how the round should be joined. It may be with a stitch, most commonly a slip stitch, or it may be with an invisible join. If it is a stitch, work the described stitch into the chain of the beginning chain stitch or stitch indicated. If the join is into the beginning chain, the chain described is the chain counting from the base of the chain—third ch of beg ch-4, is the third chain counting from the base of the chain, and the chain below the top chain of the beg ch-4. Work the joining stitch under both loops of the stitch or chain.

Invisible join

Some designers prefer to use the invisible join to join all the rounds but it is most commonly used on striped projects, when the join may be visible, and to finish the final round of a motif or project.

1 Work the end of the round, with the hook still in the last loop, cut the yarn, leaving about a 4" (10 cm) tail. Use the hook to enlarge the loop on the hook, and draw the yarn tail all the way through the top of the last stitch made.

2 Thread the yarn tail through a yarn needle. Insert the needle under both loops of the second stitch of the round. This is the stitch after a beginning chain, which counts as the first stitch.

3 Insert the needle between the top loops of the last stitch made and through the third loop behind the stitch. Draw the yarn through the fabric and to create a "false" stitch. Do not pull the yarn too tight. You want this "false" stitch to be more or less the same size as the other stitches.

4 To secure this stitch, insert the needle from top to bottom into the third loop behind the stitch and weave in the end.

Joining Yarn

Here are some tricks and tips that will help as you work on your project. They are techniques that you will encounter in some of the patterns, but they may also be useful when the unexpected happens, for example if you unexpectedly find a knot or defect in the yarn.

JOINING NEW YARN AND CHANGING COLORS

This method can be used to join a new color or a new ball of yarn at the beginning or the middle of a row or round.

1 You will need to change the color on the last yarn-over of the last stitch before the color change. In other words, stop when there are two loops left on the hook. (see above)

2 Release the old yarn and pick up the new yarn. Draw the new color through both loops to complete the stitch and continue as normal.

JOINING NEW YARN INTO THE TOP OF A STITCH

This method is used to join a new yarn to the top of a stitch after the previous stitch has been fastened off or the edge has been finished with an invisible join (see page 131). Insert the hook under the top loops of the stitch indicated in the pattern, wrap the yarn around the hook, draw the yarn loop through the fabric, and work a chain stitch to secure the yarn. Then work any chain stitches described in the pattern and continue as directed.

FASTENING OFF

When you have made the last stitch, cut the yarn about 4" (10 cm) from the work. Pull on the hook to create a large loop and then remove the hook. Thread the tail of yarn through this loop. Draw the yarn tight to fasten off—it will create a little knot.

Finishing

Like starting a project, this stage should not be rushed. It is a time to carefully prepare the project for its new life—as an object you will use and treasure or to present to someone else. The crochet stage may be over but the same care should be taken in these final steps.

BLOCKING

Even though you may have loved making the project, along the way your crochet pieces were probably stuffed into bags at some point between crochet sessions. Sometimes a pattern will state that motifs or completed projects require blocking, but every project will benefit from some form of blocking—it makes sewing the individual pieces together much easier and creates a neat finish. You can either wet block or steam block.

Wet blocking

This method is suitable for all types of yarn.

1 With the right side facing up, pin the motif or piece to the size specified in the pattern. If the size isn't specified, pin the motif or piece out so that the fabric is taut but not too stretched and the shape resembles the final shape required.

2 Put some water in a spray bottle and spray the motifs or piece with cold water until it is damp but not wet. Allow the pieces to dry completely before removing the pins.

Steam blocking

Steam blocking is best suited to natural fibers such as wool and cotton. It can also be used for synthetic fibers such as acrylic, but it is very easy to accidentally over-steam (or melt) acrylic fiber.

1 With the wrong side facing up, pin the motif or pieces out on the ironing board to the size specified in the pattern. If the size isn't specified, pin the motif or piece out so that the fabric is taut but not too stretched and the final shape resembles the required shape. Set a clothes iron on the steam setting that is most appropriate for the yarn fiber and, with the clothes iron about ½–1" (1–2.5 cm) above the work, allow the steam to penetrate the fibers without the iron actually touching the work.

2 Leave to dry for at least 30 minutes and then remove the pins.

SEAMING AND JOINING

Projects may be seamed using crochet stitches, such as slip stitch, worked through the loops along both edges to be joined, or they may be sewn together. If the pattern indicates a preferred method of seaming then it is wise to follow the instructions, but the two methods on the following pages are interchangeable. In both cases, seaming is easier if the work has been blocked first and the environment is bright and relaxed. Some people like to use the yarn tails for seaming as this reduces the number of ends to be woven in and the resulting risk of unsightly distortions in the fabric. Others prefer to use a new length of yarn and weave the yarn ends into the seam wherever possible. Choose the best method for your project.

Whipstitch

This sewing stitch works really well along both straight and curved edges. It produces a light-weight, flexible seam. Use matching yarn and a blunt yarn or tapestry needle.

1 With the right sides together, insert the needle from front to back into the front loop of the first stitch (the loop closest to you). Insert the needle from front to back into the back loop of the corresponding stitch of the other piece (the loop farthest away from you). Draw the yarn through the crochet fabric. (see above)
2 Working into the front loop only of the piece closest to you, and the back loop only of the piece farthest away from you, continue sewing the corresponding stitches along the edge—drawing the yarn tightly after every stitch.

Slip stitch

This stitch works well on straight edges or edges with an equal number of stitches, such as bag panels or cushion edges. It produces a heavy-weight, firmer seam. Use matching or contrasting yarn, and a crochet hook the same size as the one used to work the project.
1 With the right sides facing down, and the two pieces butted together, insert the hook between the top loops of the stitch on the left edge and then the corresponding stitch on the other edge. Wrap the yarn around the hook and draw the yarn through both fabrics. Repeat to the end of the seam.

Weaving in yarn tails

The project is never complete until you have secured all the loose yarn ends. You will need a blunt yarn or tapestry needle and a pair of scissors.

Thread the tapestry needle with the tail of yarn. Working on the wrong side of the fabric, thread the needle through at least 2" (5 cm) of stitches. Pull the yarn through all the way. Working in the opposite direction, skip the first stitch, and insert the needle back into the same stitches again. Skipping the first stitch is essential, because it gives the yarn something to grip on to. Pull the yarn through again. Cut the yarn close to the work. If you have done this neatly, the tails won't be visible on the front of the work. Wherever possible, work yarn ends into the seam between joined edges.

AFTERCARE

Now that you have completed the project, it is important to take care of it in the future.

* If you have used acrylic yarn for the projects, caring for them is quite straightforward. You can wash projects in the washing machine and dry them as you would any other easy-care garment. You might find that the pieces start pilling after a couple of uses or washes. This is easily remedied by running a dry shaving razor over the surface to get rid of any pilling. Be gentle if you decide to do this, as you just want to remove pilling, not shave the actual yarn.

* Do not use a clothes iron on the pieces as this may ruin the fabric drape and elasticity.

* If you have used plant fibers such as cotton or linen, wash and dry as you would any garment. You may use a clothes iron on the work if you wish.

* If you have used animal fibers, such as wool, wash the items by hand and roll them in a towel to remove most of the moisture. Then lay them out flat to dry, shaping as required. If you notice any pilling, gently scrape a dry razor over the surface to remove the pilling. Woolen items tend to pill less as time passes—unlike acrylic items, which may keep on pilling.

Tips for Using Fabric

What color do you want to use? Does it need to be the same color as the work, or would a complimentary color enrich the project?

* Once you have decided which fabric to use, you will need to decide how much of it you will need. Read the pattern instructions carefully, they will tell you the minimum amount required—including seam allowances.

* Before you cut the fabric, wash and iron the fabric and ensure that you have read the instructions correctly. Seam allowances have been included in the measurements if they are required. If you are using felt, you won't need to include a seam allowance, as felt does not fray.

* Cut out the pieces using sharp scissors or a rotary cutter and cutting mat.

* Align the edges carefully and stitch the pieces together using the suggested seam allowances.

* Press the seams flat after each seam has been stitched.

A finished project will hold memories in its very fabric. Each time you hold this project in the future you will remember where you sat, what people said during the days you worked, and what you thought about as you crocheted. The project will continue this magic throughout its life. This is just the beginning.

How to Read a Pattern

A crochet pattern may look daunting at first glance but it is a logical series of instructions, written as succinctly as possible, which aims to provide you with all the information you need. There are several different approaches to this task, and it is always worth checking which approach each pattern or publication is taking.

Each crochet pattern includes information about the materials, gauge, measurements, and finished size, as well as step-by-step instructions and abbreviations. It is a good idea to read a pattern from start to finish before you start a project. The instructions are given in the order you need them and, in order to give you the information as quickly as possible, sometimes without explanation. A seemingly strange instruction may not be an error and will make sense if you work to the end of the pattern.

PUNCTUATION

The patterns use standard abbreviations and simple punctuation.

( ) Round brackets provide additional information about a statement in the pattern. For example, "(12 dc)" listed at the end of a row, indicates that you should have worked 12 double crochet stitches in the row just completed. "Ch3 (counts as first dc)" explains that the three beginning chains count as a double crochet stitch and the stitch is included in the stitch count at the end of the row or round. Round brackets may also be used to group a repeat instruction that contains a pair of square brackets.

[ ] Square brackets may describe a set of stitch instructions, such as: "[1dc, ch3, 1dc] into the next st." This means that you will double crochet, chain 3, double crochet all in the same stitch. Square brackets may also describe a stitch repeat: "[1dc into next st, ch3, 1dc into base of last dc] twice." For this, you will double crochet, chain 3, double crochet into the next stitch and then

repeat the stitch sequence in the following stitch. This could also be written: "([1dc, ch3, 1dc] into the next st) twice." Here the rounded brackets have been used to describe the repeat of a square bracketed statement. The number of repeats indicated after a bracketed repeat is the total number of repeats.

✳ An asterisk indicates a longer pattern repeat on a row or round which you should work as you read the instruction. For example: "✳1dc, ch1, skip next st; rep from ✳ 4 times more to last st, 1dc into each of next 2 sts." This instruction tells you to double crochet, chain 1, skip the next stitch. Repeat this four more times, and then double crochet into each of the last 2 stitches. As these repeats are worked, the number of repeats indicated after an asterisk repeat is one less than the total number of repeats. So once you have read the repeat and worked it, you need to read through the repeat and work it, in this case, four more times.

- Hyphens, describe groups of stitches. Ch-3, indicates a chain of stitches 3 stitches long.

, Commas, separate the short instructions.

; Semi-colons, separate longer instructions.

Space between a number and an abbreviated description is used to indicate spans and groups of stitches. "2dc" without a space between the 2 and the dc, indicates that 2dc stitches are worked in the same position. "1dc into each of next 2 sts" indicates two single double crochet stitches worked into two different positions.

Abbreviations

Standard abbreviations have been used in this book and are listed below. Any abbreviations that are exclusive to one pattern are explained at the start of the pattern.

*	Repeat instructions between asterisks the amount of times specified	foll	following
[ ]	Repeat instructions between parentheses the amount of times specified	hdc	half double crochet
		MC	main color
approx.	approximately	mm	millimeters
beg	beginning	patt	pattern
CC	contrast color	pm	place marker
CCa	contrast color (a)	rep	repeat
CCb	contrast color (b)	rev sc	reverse single crochet
CCc	contrast color (c)	sc	single crochet
ch	chain	sc2tog	single crochet 2 sts together
cm	centimeters	sh	shade
dc	double crochet	sl st	slip stitch
dc2tog	double crochet 2 sts together	sp	space
dc3tog	double crochet 3 sts together	st(s)	stitch(es)
dec	decrease	tr	treble crochet
		yrh	yarn around hook

Meet the Designers

The projects in this book have been designed by a talented group of crafters, all eager to share the wellness benefits of crochet. Find out more about them here and by visiting their personal websites and blogs.

BETSAN CORKHILL

Well-being coach and craft expert Betsan Corkhill is a leading advocate of the power of craft as a therapeutic tool. Passionate about the whole-person approach to health, Betsan's background as a physiotherapist has enabled her to combine coaching with her medical knowledge to help individuals develop personalized well-being plans. In 2005, Betsan founded the community interest company Stitchlinks, which has since grown into a global online community for those who enjoy the therapeutic benefits of craft and is pioneering research into these benefits. Her first book, *Knit for Health and Wellness,* was published in 2014 to five-star reviews, and Betsan was recently named one of the 2015 Women of Achievement. Follow her blog at betsan.org.

ERIN BLACK

A knitter and crocheter for more than 25 years, Erin learned to love yarn by scrutinizing her granny-made afghans and toque hats that arrived promptly every Christmas. With sketchbooks filled with designs, she uses her training in design and fine arts to update a traditional craft. Find her on Etsy at midknits or on her website at midknits.com.

ALI CAMPBELL

Ali Campbell learned to crochet the hard way in the seventies, with a very fine hook and crochet cotton. Now living in Dorset, England, with her husband, two rescue dogs, several ducks, and two cows, Ali's passion is teaching this versatile and therapeutic craft to others. Alongside running her popular crochet classes, Ali has designed an online crochet course and contributes unique patterns to leading UK crochet magazines. She is the author of *Crochet for Beginners Who Want to Improve.* You can find out more about Ali on gethookedoncrochet.co.uk.

REBEKAH DESLOGE

When asked how she finds time to crochet with four kids at home, Rebekah's response is that it is her therapy. She finds time to sneak in a few rounds or rows throughout her days and finds great purpose in it. Rebekah lives in Seattle, Washington, with her husband and children. Visit her website yourmomdesigns.com and Etsy shop yourmomdesigns.

LISA GUTIERREZ

Lisa crochets from her home in Houston, Texas, where she lives with her husband and two children. She has been crocheting and knitting for about 10 years. Keep up with her and enjoy some of her other designs and patterns on her blog at goodknits.com.

CARMEN HEFFERNAN

Living in the Irish countryside, Carmen is passionate about crochet and color and feels driven to create every day. She has had designs published in *Boho Crochet* and featured in *MollieMakes*. Carmen loves to teach crochet and to inspire others to express themselves with hooks and yarn. See more crochet creations on Instagram at anniedesigncrochet and visit her Etsy shop, AnnieDesign.

NGUYEN LE

Taught to sew by her mother at a young age, Nguyen developed a love of crafting early on. She's a self-taught knitter, crocheter, needle felter, and embroiderer. Nguyen is the designer and creator of her online shop KnitKnit, and is the author of *500 Fun Little Toys* and *Color Knitting with Confidence*. She lives in Brooklyn, New York, where she can be found gulping down copious amounts of tea and cookies. Find her at knitknitknits.com.

CAROL MELDRUM

Carol has had a passion for textiles since she was a child and went on to study the subject at art school. Since graduating, she has been working as a freelance textile designer for both knit and crochet. Carol enjoys nothing better than passing on her skills and ideas through workshops across the United Kingdom, offering hands-on advice through teaching and demonstrations. She is the author of various textile books and has contributed designs to a number of joint projects and magazines. Carol is based in Glasgow, Scotland, where she can be found—in between workshops and designing—indulging in her second passion: running.

ELIZABETH PARDUE

Introduced to crocheting by her grandmother, Elizabeth did not begin creating her own projects until years later. She believes color choices are just as important as design. A full-time social worker, she spends her free time crocheting, knitting, designing patterns, and blogging. You can find inspiration and patterns on her blog, crochetincolor.blogspot.com.

DEDRI UYS

Designer of Sophie's Universe and author of *Amamani Puzzle Balls*, Dedri is passionate about crochet and shares her love of the craft through online patterns and tutorials. She lives in London, England with her husband, three sons, and the family cat. She also works as a radiotherapist. Find her patterns on Ravelry or visit her website lookatwhatimade.net.

MICAH YORK

Micah York designs crochet patterns from her home in Newport, Pennsylvania, where she lives with her husband and two children. She loves to bring joy to her family through her crafty endeavors. Making things makes her happy, so she writes crochet patterns for imaginative and playful designs that will bring a bit of extra fun to the creative lives of others. Her designs can be found at micahmakes.com.

Yarns Used in This Book

Calming Mandalas

Debbie Bliss Baby Cashmerino: 55% merino wool, 33% acrylic, 12% cashmere; 1¾ oz/50 g; 137 yds/125 m.
1 ball of each: sh71 Pool; sh204 Baby Blue; sh70 Royal.

Comforting Pillow

Lion Brand Wool-Ease Thick & Quick: 80% acrylic, 20% wool; 6 oz/170 g; 106 yds/97 m.
2 balls of MC sh110 Navy.
1 ball of each: CCa sh105 Glacier; CCb sh106 Sky Blue; CCc sh114 Denim.

Radiating Mandalas

Lion Brand Superwash Merino: 100% superwash merino wool; 3½ oz/100 g; 306 yds/280 m.
1 ball of each: CCa sh139 Peony; CC2b sh103 Coral; CCc sh170 Dijon; CCd sh157 Citron; CCe sh098 Ivory.

Sun Salutation Yoga Mat Bag

Lion Brand Superwash Merino: 100% superwash merino wool;

3½ oz/100 g; 306 yds/280 m.
1 ball of each: CCa sh157 Citron; CCb sh103 Coral; CCc sh112 Dahlia; CCd sh178 Teal; CCe sh111 Midnight Blue.

Wave Wrap

Debbie Bliss Baby Cashmerino: 55% merino wool, 33% acrylic, 12% cashmere; 1¾ oz/50 g; 137 yds/125 m.
2 balls of CCa sh58 Dark Gray.
1 ball of each: CCb sh207 Indigo; CCc sh27 Denim; CCd sh203 Teal; CCe sh57 Mist; CCf sh 202 Light Blue; CCg sh09 Slate; CCh sh65 Clotted Cream.

Meditation Seat Pillow

Lion Brand Wool-Ease: 80% acrylic, 20% wool; 3 oz/85 g; 197 yds/180 m.
3 balls of sh098 Heathered Cream.

Sleep Tight Eye Mask Set

For Eye Mask: Debbie Bliss Baby Cashmerino: 55% merino wool, 33% acrylic, 12% cashmere;

1¾ oz/50 g; 137 yds/125 m.
1 ball of each: CCa sh204 Baby Blue; CCb sh95 Cyclamen.
For Eye Mask Pouch: Debbie Bliss Baby Cashmerino: 55% merino wool, 33% acrylic, 12% Cashmere; 1¾ oz/50 g; 137 yds/125 m.
1 ball of each: CCa sh204 Baby Blue; CCb sh95 Cyclamen; CCc sh93 Clematis; CCd sh87 Damson.

Safe Document Wallet

Debbie Bliss Rialto Chunky: 100% wool; 1¾ oz/50 g; 65 yds/60 m.
2 balls of CCa sh07 Gold.
1 ball of each: CCb sh34 Jade 34; CCc sh13 Amethyst 13; CCd sh12 Navy.

No Stress Balls

Debbie Bliss Baby Cashmerino: 55% merino wool, 33% acrylic, 12% cashmere; 1¾ oz/50 g; 137 yds/125 m.
1 ball of each: CCa sh92 Orange; CCb sh78 Lipstick Pink; CCc

sh99 Sea Green; CCd sh93 Clematis; CCe sh83 Butter; CCf sh71 Pool; CCg sh02 Apple; CCh sh100 White; CCi sh06 Candy Pink; CCj sh86 Coral.

Colorful Coasters

Debbie Bliss Baby Cashmerino: 55% merino wool, 33% acrylic, 12% cashmere; 1¾ oz/50 g; 137 yds/125 m.
1 ball of each: CCa sh92 Orange; CCb sh78 Lipstick Pink; CCc sh99 Sea Green; CCd sh93 Clematis; CCe sh83 Butter; CCf sh71 Pool; CCg sh02 Apple; CCh sh100 White; CCi sh06 Candy Pink; CCj sh86 Coral.

Follow Your Heart Wall Hanging

Debbie Bliss Cotton DK: 100% cotton; 1¾ oz/50 g; 93 yds/85 m.
1 ball of MC sh02 Ecru.
1 ball of each: CCa sh073 Candy; CCb sh075 Mustard; CCc sh009 Duck Egg; CCd sh076 Marine; CCe sh051 Denim; CCf sh074 Mallow; CCg sh039 Teal.

Blue Sky Afghan

King Cole Merino blend DK:
100% wool; 1¾ oz/50 g;
123 yds/112 m.
For Baby Afghan: 10 balls of MC
sh018 Saxe; 1 ball of CC sh001
White.
For Crib Afghan: 16 balls of MC
sh018 Saxe; 2 balls of CC sh001
White.
For Lap Afghan: 23 balls of MC
sh018 Saxe; 3 balls of CC sh001
White.

Everlasting Lap Afghan

Lion Brand Wool-Ease: 80%
acrylic, 20% wool; 3 oz/85 g;
197 yds/180 m.
3 balls of CCa sh099 Fisherman.
2 balls of CCb sh111 Navy.
2 balls of CCc sh123 Seaspray.
1 ball of CCd sh114 Denim.

Hexagonal Rug

Lion Brand Wool-Ease Thick &
Quick: 80% acrylic, 20% wool;
6 oz/170 g; 106 yds/97 m.
3 balls of each: CCa sh46 Fig;
CCb sh132 Lemon Grass.
2 balls of CCc sh147 Eggplant.

Bold Bunting

Debbie Bliss Baby Cashmerino:
55% merino wool, 33% acrylic,
12% cashmere; 1¾ oz/50 g;
137 yds/125 m.
2 balls of CCa sh86 Coral.
1 ball of CCb sh99 Sea Green.

Vibrant Layered Necklace

Debbie Bliss Baby Cashmerino:
55% merino wool, 33% acrylic,
12% cashmere; 1¾ oz/50 g;
137 yds/125 m.
Oddments of each: CCa sh91
Acid Yellow; CCb sh100 White;
Ccc sh99 Sea Green; Ccd sh86
Coral.

Wake Up Happy Washcloths

Rico Creative Cotton Aran:
100% cotton; 1¾ oz/50 g;
93 yds/85 m.
1 ball of each: MC sh80 White;
CCa sh63 Light Yellow.

Spread the Love Hairclips

Scheepjeswol Cotton 8:
100% cotton; 1¾ oz/50 g;
186 yds/170 m.
Oddments of each: CCa sh722

Ochre; CCb sh653 Dark Pink;
CCc sh501 Natural; CCd sh663
Light Pastel Green; CCe sh642
Light Green; CCf sh719 Pink;
CCg sh718 Light Pink.

Friendship Quilt

Debbie Bliss Cashmerino Aran:
55% merino wool, 33% acrylic,
12% cashmere; 1¾ oz/50 g;
98 yds/90 m.
2 balls of each: MC sh075 Citrus;
CCa sh073 Coral; CCb sh072
Peach; CCc sh062 Kingfisher;
CCd sh061 Jade; CCe sh060
Fuchsia.

Let's Be Friends Bracelets

DMC Size 5 Pearlized Cotton
Embroidery Thread: 2 yds (2 m).
Colorways: 368; 500; 502; 725;
742; 796; 799.
Nicole Jewelry Connection Bead
It in "Carnival": size 6 glass beads
Nicole Jewelry Connection Bead
It 6mm wood bead.

Index

Acknowledgments

Thanks to the following for their help in making this book:

Our wonderful author, Betsan Corkhill, for her expertise in whole-person health and pioneering work in promoting the therapeutic benefits of craft.

Thanks also to our amazing crocheters for their contributions in designing and making the following projects:

Erin Black

Bold Bunting and Vibrant Layered Necklace

Ali Campbell

Colorful Coasters and No Stress Balls

Rebekah Desloge

Sleep Tight Eye Mask Set and Safe Document Wallet

Lisa Gutierrez

Calming Mandalas and Comforting Pillow

Carmen Heffernan

Wake Up Happy Washcloths and Spread the Love Hairclips

Nguyen Le

Radiating Mandalas and Sun Salutation Yoga Mat Bag

Carol Meldrum

Blue Sky Afghan and Follow Your Heart Wall Hanging

Elizabeth Pardue

Everlasting Lap Afghan and Hexagonal Rug

Dedri Uys

Wave Wrap and Meditation Seat Pillow

Micah York

Friendship Quilt and Let's Be Friends Bracelets

Thanks to photographer, Simon Pask, and our lovely model, Emily Slaughter at Simon How Agency, for bringing the projects to life.

Many thanks to The Romo Group for supplying the Giotto Wallcovering Lovat (as seen on pages 4, 5, 7, 15, 26, 32, 41, 44, 48, 55, 72, 77, 78, 102, 117).

Thanks also to Claire Crompton, Diana LeCore, Luise Roberts, and Abi Waters for their editorial work and index.

Thanks also to 1010 Printing International Ltd.